Keeping Your Family Grounded
When You're Flying by the Seat of Your Pants

Tim Jordan, MD

Children & Families, Inc

Keeping Your Family Grounded
When You're Flying by the Seat of Your Pants
Tim Jordan, MD
Children & Families, Inc.

Published by Children & Families, Inc., St. Louis, MO
Copyright ©2025 Tim Jordan, MD
All rights reserved.

No part of this publication may be reproduced, stored in a retrieval system, or transmitted in any form or by any means, electronic, mechanical, photocopying, recording, scanning, or otherwise, except as permitted under Section 107 or 108 of the 1976 United States Copyright Act, without the prior written permission of the Publisher. Requests to the Publisher for permission should be addressed to Permissions Department, Children & Families, Inc. and Anne@drtimjordan.com.

Limit of Liability/Disclaimer of Warranty: While the publisher and author have used their best efforts in preparing this book, they make no representations or warranties with respect to the accuracy or completeness of the contents of this book and specifically disclaim any implied warranties of merchantability or fitness for a particular purpose. No warranty may be created or extended by sales representatives or written sales materials. The advice and strategies contained herein may not be suitable for your situation. You should consult with a professional where appropriate. Neither the publisher nor author shall be liable for any loss of profit or any other commercial damages, including but not limited to special, incidental, consequential, or other damages.

Cover and Interior design: Davis Creative Publishing, DavisCreativePublishing.com

Publisher's Cataloging-in-Publication

Names: Jordan, Timothy J., 1954- author.

Title: Keeping your family grounded : when you're flying by the seat of your pants / Tim Jordan, MD.

Description: [Revised and updated edition]. | St. Louis, MO : Children & Families, Inc., [2025] | Includes bibliographical references.

Identifiers: ISBN: 978-0-9771051-5-1 (paperback) | 978-0-9771051-6-8 (ebook) | LCCN: 2025902897

Subjects: LCSH: Parenting. | Child rearing. | Parent and child. | Families. | Interpersonal communication. | BISAC: FAMILY & RELATIONSHIPS / Parenting / General. | FAMILY & RELATIONSHIPS / Life Stages / School Age. | FAMILY & RELATIONSHIPS / Marriage & Long-Term Relationships.

Classification: LCC: HQ755.8 .J67 2025 | DDC: 649.1--dc23

ATTENTION CORPORATIONS, UNIVERSITIES, COLLEGES AND PROFESSIONAL ORGANIZATIONS: Quantity discounts are available on bulk purchases of this book for educational, gift purposes, or as premiums for increasing magazine subscriptions or renewals. Special books or book excerpts can also be created to fit specific needs. For information, please contact Children & Families, Inc. 16100 Chesterfield Parkway West, Ste. 200, Chesterfield, Missouri 63017; ph 636-530-1883 or email Anne@drtimjordan.com

Dedication

This book is dedicated to my wife Anne and our own three children, Kelly, TJ and John, for all they have taught me about myself and parenting for the past 40 years.

It is also dedicated to all of my other "adopted" kids from my camps, retreats and office practice who continue to educate and inspire me about my life's work.

Acknowledgments

I would like to thank my wife, Anne, for her encouragement for all of my projects and for teaching parents together with our parenting classes and presentations

Also, a big thank you goes out to Jenny Harrell, Isa Jordan and Maria Weber for their early draft manuscript reading and editing assistance.

Table of Contents

Chapter 1 | Introduction 1
Chapter 2 | Begin with the End in Mind 9
Chapter 3 | Overindulged Children 13
Chapter 4 | The Goodwill Account 31
Chapter 5 | Listening 45
Chapter 6 | Time Together Inside 55
Chapter 7 | Time in Nature 63
Chapter 8 | Traditions and Rituals 73
Chapter 9 | Family Meetings 79
Chapter 10 | Boundaries and Discipline 85
Chapter 11 | Opportunities to Grow 89
Chapter 12 | Chores, Homework, Allowance
               and Other Everyday Matters 97
Chapter 13 | Youth Sports 107
Chapter 14 | Technology and Social Media 115
Chapter 15 | Self-Quieting 135
Chapter 16 | Staying Connected with
               Your Teenager 145
Chapter 17 | Taking Care of Yourself and
               Your Marriage 155
Chapter 18 | Odds and Ends 163
Chapter 19 | What's Really Important 171
Resources 181
About the Author 187

Chapter 1

Introduction

"Everybody today seems to be in such a terrible rush, anxious for greater developments and greater riches and so on; so that children have very little time with their parents, and parents have very little time for each other, and so in the home begins the disruption of the peace of the world."
~Mother Theresa of Calcutta

As this book approaches its 20th anniversary, I still, unfortunately, find that these wise words resonate with today's families just as they did 20 years ago. I am not an alarmist, overreacting to every story headlined in the news. But I do worry that kids today are experiencing intensified busyness and distractions.

Kids seem to be tuned in electronically but tuned out emotionally. They seem strongly attached to their "things" yet disconnected from their families and other important adults.

They are overloaded with information about celebrities, fashions and electronics yet lack self-awareness and important life skills. They are experts at being busy, involved, and distracted but struggle with being alone and quiet. They can hook up complicated computers or video game systems yet have a hard time connecting with friends and enjoying the simple pleasures in life.

Kids can connect electronically with people, ideas and cultures from around the world and yet are so overprotected that they have very few opportunities to spread their wings to explore their neighborhoods. I fear that they are overprotected in the real world yet underprotected in the digital world. They have smartphones and social media to communicate with others at will, yet are disconnected like never before in history from family members and traditions. They have access via books, TV and the internet to religions all over the globe and yet are spiritually starved.

Technologies make every person and situation pauseable and allow continuous connection but rarely our full attention. We all suffer to some degree today from a lack of depth of conversation, relationships with intimacy without privacy, and companionship that prioritizes convenience. Well before our digital age, Shakespeare summed it up perfectly: *"We are consumed with that which we are nourished."* Author Sherry Turkle has written that *"The ties we form through the Internet are not, in the end, the ties that bind. But they are the ties that preoccupy."* That pretty well sums it up.

"Laughter clubs" have been springing up all over the world. It seems that adults are so stressed, distracted, and unhappy that they actually are going to classes to remember how to laugh and have fun! There are thousands of these clubs worldwide in 120+ countries. This seems to me to be another sad testament to how out of balance, hurried, distracted and unhappy people are becoming.

Let me ask you a few questions to make sure this book is a good fit for your needs:

Do you ever feel like you and the family are rushing around nonstop to sporting events and enrichment activities, leaving precious little time to relax at home?

Do you ever wish you had more family meals together instead of eating in the car on the way to an activity?

Do you ever feel stressed out by the busyness of your life and don't know who to blame?

On Sunday nights, do you ever wonder where the week has gone?

Are you tired of trying to keep up with your children's friends and peers so that your kids don't fall behind them?

Do you find yourself tired and crabby and short with your children because you are so stressed and exhausted?

Do you find yourself engaged in recurrent power struggles with your children over chores, homework, or time on their devices and wish you could practice a different kind of discipline model that wasn't about rewards and punishment or yelling and threats?

Ever worry that you are raising spoiled, overindulged, and entitled kids?

Do you have a hard time finding a balance between keeping your kids safe while also allowing them the freedoms they need to develop confidence and resilience?

Ever worry about when to start your kids with their own phones or allow them to get on social media?

Do you worry about how to stay connected to your teenager?

Do you worry that your kids and family are losing touch with your old family traditions and rituals that were so important to you?

Would you like to learn how to make decisions about raising your children based on your values and what's important to you?

If you resonate with any of these questions, then you have come to the right place.

Keeping Your Family Grounded When You're Flying by the Seat of Your Pants will hopefully bring some sanity back into your home and family. I hope to thoughtfully stimulate your thinking about what is really important and what your kids and family really need to be happy and emotionally healthy. And I want you to take away some very practical and usable tools like the Goodwill Account deposits, family meetings, being a good listener, setting good boundaries, establishing rituals and traditions, and learning how best to introduce and manage your children's technology usage.

In this revised edition, I am adding several brand new chapters on topics including how to begin with the end in mind by proactively deciding your family's values and priorities; when and how to allow your adolescents to start with smartphones and social media; how we've shifted from a play-based childhood to a more digital-based one, including how that developed and the costs to children; the out-of-control youth sports industry and how it is harming children and families; and also a chapter on how to listen so that you can remain an influence in your children's lives throughout the teen years and beyond.

There was a study out of UCLA in 1967 showing that 86% of college freshmen around the country said that "developing a meaningful philosophy of life" was very important to them, with only 40% listing that "being very well off financially" was very important. When UCLA repeated the survey in 2003, only 40% of freshmen listed a meaningful philosophy of life as important vs. 74% saying financial security was most important. A different report on nearly 290,000 freshmen in over 500 colleges in 1988 showed a 20-year high with 75.6% interested in being very well off financially vs. a 20-year low of 39.4% in support for developing a meaningful philosophy of life. These trends over those 20 years suggest a gradual but profound shift not only in students' values but also in the values of the larger culture.

A 2023 report by the Walton Family Foundation and Gallup called the Voices of Gen Z Study (children and young adults born between 1997 and 2012) revealed information on the emotional lives of 10-18-year-old children. One finding was that more than 90% of Gen Z children felt a lot of happiness and enjoyment the prior day — but sizeable segments also felt stress (45%), anxiety (38%), anger (29%), sadness or loneliness (17%). Teen percentages, as you might expect, were higher: stress (58%), worry (43%), anxiety (47%), sadness and loneliness (24%). About one in three Gen Z kids said they felt like they had to be perfect. Parents stated that their top challenges to raising children today were fostering independence and preparing them for adult life, children's emotions, social media and technology, building strong relationships and communication, and time management. Yet, I don't find that that is where parents are most focused in their day-to-day parenting.

And then there are these sobering statistics about today's college students from the 2023 American College Health Association's National Spring Survey of 103,639 students from 154 universities. They asked students about whether or not they had experienced negative mental health symptoms most days in the past year. The following shows their high level of symptoms: anxiety-49%, burnout-41%, self-doubt-45%, sadness-37%, depression-34%, social isolation-34%, hopelessness-29%, panic attacks- 29%, suicidal thoughts-16%.

In terms of their careers, Gen Z values jobs that allow them to live comfortably (77%) and pursue their passions (70%) over becoming wealthy (31%) or managers (12%). Combined, the findings indicate a desire for balance between reaching financial stability and maintaining personal fulfillment and strong relationships. This study gives me hope that kids and young adults are shifting back to more healthy priorities.

5-year-old: I'm going to be so good tomorrow. Mom: What about today? 5-year-old: I have plans.

When I say in the title that I want to keep families grounded, I mean emotionally and spiritually. I want kids to have a more balanced life with time for fun, spontaneous play and connections with family and friends in addition to schoolwork, sports and activities.

I also want them to have time to reflect, soul search, question, and daydream. They need quiet, alone time to check in with themselves and to be in touch with their feelings and inner voice. I want them to learn to be alone without being lonely.

If you want your kids to feel grounded even as the world around them is flying by the seat of its pants, they must feel more connected at home. There needs to be more time playing with their parents and siblings. Kids need to know their parents are available to listen, validate their feelings and support them. Parents also need to establish good boundaries and hold kids accountable to them.

I am asking parents to take a good, hard, honest look at themselves, their marriage, their schedules and priorities, and the ways that they parent. This includes becoming more aware of what we are modeling for our children with how we live our lives. Kids are always a reflection of the adult world around them. You'll have the opportunity to point your finger inward to things you can take responsibility for vs. just blaming social media, the culture and our children.

Another cost of our disconnected, hectic lives is that kids are hurting a lot. Their hurts are being played out as misbehaviors and symptoms of anxiety, stress, and depression which are subsequently being labeled and medicated at an ever-increasing and alarming rate. I believe that if families were more grounded, connected and tuned in to their children's needs, a lot of kids would lose their labels and settle into healthier mental well-being.

Throughout history, parents have always worried about their kids. Each generation has had its set of fears and concerns that always reflect the tenor of the times. Each generation for the past century has also had its "parenting experts." Each new expert tended to disprove the previous expert's advice and dispense new prescriptions for parenting. All of this left parents scratching their heads in confusion. Our present generation of parents is no different, with information overload at an all-time high.

The information in this book is not meant as a cookie-cutter recipe for how-to-parenting. I hope it doesn't come across that way as you read it. I do believe parents need a wake-up call, a chance to step back from their everyday busy lives to consciously decide how they want their family to look like, feel like and behave. I say consciously because many parents today are so wrapped up in the "game" of getting ahead and trying to make their kids successful and happy that they've lost the forest (what you decide is really important) for the trees (what the culture values).

What is the tone of your home that you want to create? What kind of values and character do you want your kids to internalize as they grow up in your home? How can you fight off the negative, unhealthy cultural messages while instilling healthy long-term values and teachings in your home?

I hope this book helps you and your kids get what you want. I have lived these principles in my parenting life as well as with the kids and teens I serve in my personal growth retreats and summer camps.

Kids are hungry for deeper connections and a slower pace. I experience it first-hand at our camps. They love campfires, stargazing, silly, non-competitive games, learning self-calming skills and taking sunset walks. They love the deep connections they have with our staff and with their fellow campers.

These same feelings can be created at home. Good luck and have fun creating the family of your dreams.

Chapter 2

Begin with the End in Mind

Read this visualization and then close your eyes and experience it: *Imagine you are walking along your favorite beach, and you come upon a pier jutting out into the ocean. See yourself walking down this pier until you see a bench at the end that faces back towards the shore. Have a seat on the bench. Now imagine you see your child/children walking towards you, but I want you to imagine them at thirty years of age, all grown up. In your mind, envision them as you'd like for them to be, best case, as adults. What qualities do they live out? What kind of person are they? See yourself giving them a hug and watch as they walk back to shore. Then, open your eyes and write down what you envisioned.*

My wife and I have performed that visualization during presentations to groups of parents throughout the United States and in 16 other countries. And what is fascinating is that the list of what parents envisioned for their adult children is amazingly similar. The following are the qualities we hear regularly from parents:

Happy, healthy, fulfilled, grounded, curious, independent, compassionate, close to their family including siblings, live outside their parent's home, motivated, self-sufficient and off the dole, street smarts, good people skills, forward-thinking, service-oriented, spiritual, kind, caring, successful, have a purpose and honest. Oh, and did I say still close to their parents?

What is interesting to me is that we have NEVER had a parent list things like straight A's, winning national championships in youth sports or attending a top-tier college. Yet, where do so much of our parenting energy and worries go in our daily lives? Why do we get so frantic about wanting our kids to be popular, be selected for a traveling club soccer team, get straight A's and take pressurized AP classes, and become hell-bent on them being admitted into Ivy League universities? In a word, fear.

I have found two main fears that drive parents to do too much for their kids and to focus on unhealthy things. One is parents' fear that their children are going to fall behind their peers and not keep up or be left behind. I can't tell you how many times I have heard parents tell me they want to "Give my daughter a leg up" or "Give her an edge." In the 1950s, we used to talk about the pressure families felt to "Keep up with the Jones'". There was an explosion of new homes, appliances, cars, and television sets. If you saw your neighbor bring home a new appliance, there was pressure to go buy one to keep in the mainstream.

Today, most people own expensive tennis shoes and electronic devices. But we've shifted our fear to "Keeping up with the Jones' children." If you hear that your neighbor has signed their son up for a soccer camp in the summer or hired a professional pitching coach or been selected for a traveling club volleyball team, there is pressure to do the same for your child lest they get behind. And if they don't play on the year-round soccer team, they'll get behind their peers and not be able to make their high school team. And if they don't make their high school team, they'll never achieve a scholarship to play in college! It is *so* easy for today's parents to get wound up with these fears, and it becomes a slippery slope.

The second fear I hear from parents is the confusion about how to best prepare their kids for a future that is so different from our own experience. And a future where the kinds of jobs and skills needed for such careers are quickly and regularly changing. We seem to have lost the security of our expectations. 100 years ago, it was easy to take your son or daughter out to your farm's fields and point to the acreage they would soon be inheriting and working. No such luck today.

In response to these fears, parents try to provide a prolonged, protected period of childhood, education and preparation. It has also instigated a parenting style of overprotection, overindulging and micromanaging children's lives. Compared to previous generations, moms and dads push, pressure, rescue, problem-solve and take responsibility for their children's happiness. Parents, in turn, become overwhelmed, overworked, worry too much, and take their children's behaviors, successes and failures too personally. Parental focus veers away from keeping their end in mind qualities and outcomes into unhealthy realms.

I encourage you and your spouse to do the visualization separately and then combine your results. Stephen Covey popularized the process of beginning with the end in mind as one of the habits in his best-selling book *The 7 Habits of Highly Successful People*. Once you have your end in mind for your children, use these qualities as your guidepost whenever you make decisions about things such as signing them up for sports teams, extracurricular activities or enrichment courses. Let me share an example of how this looked in our family.

One spring, our son TJ asked us to sign him up for a spring hockey team. We had just finished up his regular hockey season, and he was set to begin spring baseball. One of the agreements our family, parents and kids had committed to was each child would only play one sport a season. One of the "ends in mind" we had come up with together was that we all valued downtime and time at home. So we reminded TJ of our agreement, and despite tears and lots of, "But everybody else on my team is playing spring hockey," we kept to our agreement. We used our end in mind, which had been conceived when we weren't feeling pressured, to guide our decision vs. making choices based on what everyone else was doing.

Let me end this chapter with a great story from author Anthony DeMello that demonstrates the rat race to nowhere that so many parents find themselves in today.

A group of tourists were traveling on a bus through the gorgeous Tuscany countryside in Italy, but surprisingly, all the shades were pulled down so that no one could see beyond the windows. The travelers spent the whole trip arguing over who got to sit in the front seat, who got to sit by the window, who was in charge and who was to be applauded. And so they remained until the journey's end.

Don't miss out on what's truly important to you and your family. Create your end in mind and use it to keep your family grounded and heading in the direction you choose.

Chapter 3

Overindulged Children

An 11-year-old boy spent a beautiful, sunny Saturday indoors playing video games. His older sister tried coaxing him outside by warning, "Someday, you're going to be 30 years old, single, and living in mom's basement playing video games all day!" His reply: "A boy can dream, can't he?"

Last spring, during a session of my high school support group, four seniors expressed intense fears about not wanting to grow up, and they brought a lot of energy and angst to the conversation. I decided to record them for an episode of my podcast, Raising Daughters, and what they shared on that recording was eye-opening. As they shared their fears, they all came to the same conclusion: the main reason for their worries was due to the fact that their parents had done too much for them growing up. Parents had performed too much problem-solving, fixing, rescuing, and hovering. The young women realized that they hadn't had enough experience doing those things for themselves and thus hadn't developed the confidence that they could make decisions and cope with the normal ups and downs of life. I think they were spot on.

Research has shown that the majority of young adults leaving the nest at eighteen years of age have never done their own laundry, learned to manage money, advocated for themselves with teachers and coaches, followed a budget, or learned to think critically and problem-solve. Teens today are putting off things like getting their driver's licenses or working a job. So it's no surprise that the 2023 Census showed that 58% of men and 54% of women aged 18 – 25 years live at home with their parents because they lack the means, financial or otherwise, to support themselves. For perspective, during the 1960s, only 24% did so. Ironically, increased college education and later marriages might explain why more women are living at home today. Based on my podcast conversation, I would add that they also lack the street smarts, confidence, and self-reliance to launch out into the world.

I mentioned in the last chapter that parents today tend to overprotect and overindulge their children. I find that most people equate being overindulged with kids receiving too many toys and devices and becoming overly materialistic. But there are many faces of being overindulged, and the following are the ones I see most often.

What Does Overindulged Mean?

1. **No delayed gratification** – Kids have become used to being constantly entertained and given what they want when they want it (which is usually now!). So it's no surprise that they have a hard time delaying gratification. It doesn't help that their time spent playing video games and on social media has conditioned them to expect immediate fulfillment. Kids have become so impatient that they scream at their computer screens if there is a 2-second delay in information coming up. Umm, that last example includes me and most adults as well.

2. **Entertaining kids** – Many parents take way too much responsibility for entertaining their kids. Overindulged kids tend to get bored quickly and often. Things don't mean as much to you if you don't have some investment in them (hard work, financial, waiting for it). Kids learn to look to their parents to entertain them because their parents have been all too willing to fill the voids. Parents don't like to see their kids unhappy, and so they become their children's entertainment directors.

When I was bored my mom yelled at us to go outside and figure it out, which we did.

3. **High-Intensity experiences** – Our whole culture has lost the ability to do more with less—to enjoy the simple pleasures in life. Kids have become addicted to visual-motor thrills from so much time with video games, computer games, television, paintball, movies, walking through malls, skateboard ramps and scrolling through social media sites. This is another reason why they get bored so often and so easily. They develop an intense need for intense stimulation.

4. **Insatiability** – Because kids get so much so soon and because they have been exposed to intoxicating levels of intense stimulation, entertainment and gratification, it's easy to understand why their appetites become so large for the above. The desire for stimulation, material things and intense experiences become cravings, and kids are conditioned to believe that they can't be happy without these things. And no matter what they have, it's never enough. They become insatiable.

It's hard to feel "full" when your life has been so full of fun and games that are given to you without any effort on your own part or having to wait for them. Everything around kids is "fast": fast food, computers, video games, communicating with friends via cell phones. Kids learn when they get bored to quickly seek out their next thrill, and they usually get it.

5. **Social interactions** – Kids and adults today have a hard time being alone, especially being alone without feeling lonely. We've become so used to being busy and distracted. Many kids are constantly hooked up with their friends. Even when they come home from being out with friends, they have continuous connections through cell phones and social media.

Unfortunately, those online connections are not as deep or meaningful as face-to-face interactions.

6. **Praise/rewards** – Our generation of parents seems to have gone overboard in trying to be sure our kids are happy and have high self-esteem. And we've mistakenly felt that filling kids up with externals will do that. Too many princes and princesses have been put up on pedestals their whole lives and told how great they are. They've been performing for adults, i.e., parents, coaches, and teachers since they were in preschool, and learned to crave people constantly rooting for them. Kids become addicted to praise and often get caught up in unhealthy cycles of pleasing others, striving for others' approval, and needing their drugs of praise to feel good about themselves. Kids become way too dependent on externals (rewards, money, bribes, praise) to motivate them.

7. **Materialism** – Kids have way too many things, i.e., toys, video games, clothes, or the latest fad. They've bought the cultural lie that what makes you happy is acquiring more things. Many homes even need a "toy room" to fit all of the stuff parents and grandparents have bought kids. Children are constantly bombarded with advertising on TV, movies and social media, which feeds their appetites. Even little preschoolers today are dressed in designer clothes and have tablets and televisions in their rooms.

8. **Do too much for kids** – Comedian Melanie Reno jokes "I got my 1st full-time job, but I could have sworn I was making more money in college, working for my parents as their daughter."

    I talk more about this in Chapter 11 but suffice it to say that we tend to do too much for kids today. Parents get too involved in their children's friendship troubles, homework, and conflicts with teachers and coaches. Many kids don't have chores or responsibilities at home. We overprotect kids in hopes of preventing mistakes and suffering. We solve their problems for them, talk for them and walk behind them, sweeping up their messes and mistakes.

The mistakes we are not allowed to make growing up we will make as adults, with less benefit and more suffering.

9. **Supervision** – This area will also be flushed out in Chapter 11. Kids get so much of their everyday structure from without that they rarely have to organize themselves, prioritize, create their own routines, entertain themselves or initiate anything. Kids are constantly performing for and being judged by adults (parents, teachers, coaches, peers) through academics, sports and their social lives, creating relentless pressure on them to impress everyone. This leaves precious little time for self-assessment, self-exploration and self-motivation.

10. **Activities** – I described the phenomenon of trying to keep up with the Jones' children in chapter 2, and this results in an excess of activities. Kids whine and complain until their parents allow them to join the indoor soccer team, even though they are at the same time playing ice hockey and fall baseball. Because parents can't say no, families spend most of their weekday afternoons, evenings and weekends frantically rushing from one event to the next, leaving little time for family meals together, downtime and family time. Parents fear if they don't get their kids into all these activities that they will fall behind their peers and so the merry-go-round keeps spinning out of control. This becomes the proverbial race to nowhere.

11. **Fitting in** – Being popular, looking good and fitting in have become way too important in our culture. So much so that parents are willing to buy their kids expensive designer clothes

and shoes, hairstyles and colorings, or whatever else is "popular" at that moment. Whether you're talking paintball guns, skateboards, basketball shoes, prom dresses, or the recent trend of plastic surgery, parents cave into their children's relentless badgering for the latest cool "in" thing.

12. **Work** – Too many kids are given something for nothing. Many kids today don't know from experience the meaning of hard work and diligence. Kids don't need to work hard or fulfill expectations to get what they want; they just get it! They haven't experienced the rewards that come from self-sacrifice, perseverance and working one's way up the ladder of success. For many kids, good grades, athletic achievement and popularity have come so easily that they've never struggled and had to overcome hardships or obstacles.

    This issue is perhaps best described by a story about an entitled grade school boy who, when asked by his teacher which book had helped him the most in his life, answered, "My father's checkbook."

13. **Wasted time** – Kids are allowed to spend an inordinate amount of time doing unproductive things, i.e. video games, texting, social media sites, YouTube videos, or streaming television series. This unfocused, disengaged time doesn't produce any useful result or skill and, for many kids, comprises much of their non-school time.

14. **Not taking responsibility** – Parents take on way too much responsibility for their children's entertainment, school work, mistakes, stress, frustrations, problem-solving and happiness. Kids respond by doing a lot of blaming, denying, overreacting, falling apart, exploding, experiencing physical symptoms (stomachaches, headaches), avoiding, not taking risks and giving up whatever they aren't good at. In essence, they

don't take responsibility for their lot in life—their relationship issues, school work, feelings and happiness. Oftentimes, the ways they inappropriately react to their problems become more problematic than the initial difficulty was.

Why Parents Overindulge Kids

I guess the next question to ask ourselves is "Why are kids so overindulged today?" "Why have we, as parents, allowed it to happen?" The following are some reasons why.

1. **There is more to want today.** Kids are exposed to these things more often and more intensely via advertising on television, movies, and social media. The average teenager sees about 20,000 commercials every year. During Saturday morning cartoon time, kids are exposed to one food ad every 5 minutes. And kids as young as the preschool years are targeted by marketers of food, games and clothing.

   Plus, there are so many more brands of shoes, streaming apps, opportunities to access movies and music, fast food choices in school cafeterias, and ways to access movie stars and sports stars 24/7. Kids are inundated with images of what's cool all day long.

2. **Poor boundary setting.** Many of this generation's parents don't want to repeat the authoritarian parenting style of their parents—criticism, yelling, spanking, comparing. Yet, they don't know how to set good boundaries and follow through without the old ways. So many parents today don't follow through consistently and have a hard time saying no to their kids' cravings and demands.

3. **Working parent guilt.** This is one culprit of the hard-to-set-boundaries camp, especially when both parents work outside the home. With so little time together, parents want

the time with their children to be conflict-free and happy, so they tend to give in more to keep the peace. Giving in and buying kids things helps to assuage parental guilt from not having much time together. Tired, drained parents also don't have the patience and fortitude to stick to their guns when their kids push the limits; it's easier in the short run to give in, although, in the long run, they've created a monster.

4. **Fear: It's never a good idea to parent out of fear.** But parents today fear their kids might fall behind their peers when it comes to academics and the pursuit of college scholarships, youth select sports teams that result in spots in high school sports and subsequent college scholarships, and the social ladder climbing that results in popularity. They get caught up in comparing their kids to their peers and in the endless competitions rampant in school, sports, dance, cheerleading or whatever is popular at the time. Again, it's about keeping up with the Jones' children.

5. **Feeling responsible for their children's happiness.** As mentioned previously, I think parents have gotten caught up in taking too much responsibility for their children's happiness. And being happy by current cultural definition means more "things," more activities and more notoriety. It also means being happy all of the time with no sadness, uncertainty, or disappointments. So parents do too much, give too much and care too much (i.e., care more than their kids about homework, fitting in, sports teams, etc.).

6. **Suffering and unhappiness.** We've become overly concerned about our children's happiness and self-esteem. And we've mistakenly decided that it's our job as parents to prevent suffering and hardship—to protect our kids from the harsh realities that life brings naturally. We've forgotten that

frustration, making mistakes and suffering are the breeding ground for building character. Self-pride results from overcoming obstacles on your own so that you can say to yourself, "I did it!" A sense of honor and confidence is earned by handling your mistakes and being in charge of your own life and happiness.

Costs to Overindulged Kids

A man pleaded with his psychiatrist, "You've got to help me, it's my son." Psychiatrist: "What's the matter with him?" Dad, "He's always eating mudpies. I get up in the morning and there he is in the yard eating mudpies. I come home at lunch and he's eating mudpies. I come home at dinner and he's in the backyard eating mudpies." The psychiatrist tried to reassure the man, "Give him some time, it's all a part of growing up." Dad: "Well, I don't like it, and neither does his wife!"

1. **Sense of entitlement:** Feeling that you should always get what you want whenever you want it and without effort or self-sacrifice does not work well out in the real world. It causes major disturbances in friendships, marriages and in the workplace. There are a lot of depressed twenty-somethings who feel entitled to success and glory yet have no clue how it works in life. They don't understand the concept of starting at the bottom rung and working their way up to the top.

   The world does not owe them a living, and nothing will be handed to them on a silver platter. It's a steep learning curve for pampered young adults when the harsh realities of the real world hit them after college.

   A dad I met once said that as his wife and he were sitting at the dining room table one evening discussing their finances, their entitled 15-year-old son walked in, saw what they were doing, and glibly asked his parents, "Heh, guys, how are we doing with the finances?" His dad looked up and quickly retorted, "Actually, your mom and I are doing great. You, on the other hand, are broke!" I love that story.

2. **Poor coping skills:** Overindulged kids haven't learned how to manage stress, problem solve, resolve conflicts, negotiate through impasses, deal with feelings of frustration, uncertainty, and inadequacy, or deal with the normal ups and downs of relationships, work and life. They lack perseverance and resiliency.

3. **Lack of motivation and ambition:** High levels of immediate gratification and stimulation can drain anyone's motivation and ambition. It makes it difficult to accept that you can't have the corner office, leadership position, or the big house and six-week vacation when you start your career. It also makes it hard to follow a budget and not run up huge credit card debts. And it makes you very difficult to live with or work with. The following story demonstrates this problem perfectly.

A very successful businessman had a meeting with his new son-in-law. "I love my daughter, and now I welcome you into the family. To show you how much we care for you, I'm making you a 50/50 partner in my business. All you have to do is go to the factory every day and learn the operations." The son-in-law interrupted, "I hate factories; I can't stand the noise." "I see," replied the father. "Well then, you can start working in the office and take charge of some of the operations there." The new son-in-law quickly interrupted, "I hate office work, I can't stand being stuck behind a desk all day." "Wait a minute", said the father-in-law. "I just made you half-owner of a money-making organization, but you don't like factories and won't work in the office. What am I going to do with you?" "Easy," said the young man. "Buy me out."

4. **Cravings:** Overindulged kids become teenagers and adults who are addicted to praise, high-intensity stimulation, material things, fitting in, winning and being the best. This creates a constant tension within people—Am I going to get my "drugs?" and "If I get them, will I be able to keep them? And, of course, as the great philosopher Mick Jagger once sang, "You can't always get what you want," so you've set yourself up for feeling empty and frustrated. This increases your cravings and needs for those "things," and thus, the unhealthy cycle continues. Overindulged kids grow up to become insatiable, discontented, and insufferable adults.

5. **Self-responsible:** If you've been consistently and constantly entertained, supervised and protected, you haven't developed any of the internal structures necessary to become self-sufficient. You haven't learned how to organize yourself, prioritize activities, handle your own conflicts and challenges, make decisions based on your internal compass, or initiate, create and direct your life. I've met a lot of adults who remain stuck whining and blaming and who never learned to take responsibility for their own happiness.

6. **Self-Knowledge:** The way to get to know yourself, to define yourself, and to have a sense of direction that fits for you is through lots of quiet time thinking, reflecting, soul searching, and daydreaming. Self-knowledge comes through testing yourself, monitoring yourself and being true to yourself. It comes from having opportunities to learn and grow, as described in Chapter 11. It develops from learning from mistakes and failures as well as successes. It means being comfortable being alone and spending time with yourself.

Overindulged kids haven't taken the time for this self-exploration, having spent most of their time and energy with busyness, stimulating entertainment, proving themselves, performing, and being cool and popular.

7. **Life skills:** Most overindulged children haven't learned the essential skills needed out in the real world of work and adult relationships. I'm talking about skills such as conflict resolution, critical thinking, self-monitoring, self-motivation, negotiation, delayed gratification, long-term vision, creating your own structure and routines, managing stress, charting your own course, and hard work and commitment to excellence no matter what the task is. So these kids start out their adult life with major deficits that are hard to make up.

8. **Eternal adolescence:** Finally, many young adults, like my high school group seniors, seem trapped in adolescence, fearful to venture out into the adult world. Thus, we have a constantly enlarging population of twenty-somethings moving back home, postponing tough career choices, enrolling in graduate school for unclear reasons, and having a hard time coming to grips emotionally, socially and psychologically with what it takes to be happily married, happily employed and to be grown up.

Life Lessons Kids Need to Learn

I've already alluded to a lot of these lessons, but let me list several of them as a reminder.

1. Delayed gratification, focus on the long-term.
2. Value of hard work and self-sacrifice.
3. You are responsible for your motivation, validation, feelings, resolving conflicts, making up for your mistakes and clearing up your messes.
4. Learning to save and budget money.
5. Filling yourself up with healthy fillers vs. thrills.

6. Slow down, self-quiet and look within for your answers, to access your intuition, and to know yourself.
7. Becoming a critical thinker and problem solver.
8. Lead, initiate, create, take risks, strategize, challenge and test yourself.
9. Develop coping skills.
10. Set your own bar and create your own expectations for yourself.
11. Know what's really important in life: close relationships, doing fulfilling work that you love, being of service, being a good spouse, parent, friend.

What Can Parents Do?

There is much that parents can do to both prevent overindulgence and provide opportunities for kids to learn important life skills.

1. **Your presence is invaluable.** What they really want and need from us is our undivided time, our love, and to be heard, understood and accepted for who they are.

   There are tons of ways to show we care that aren't about giving "things." Review the deposits for the Goodwill Account in Chapter 4, as those are just what the doctor ordered.

2. **Teach kids to problem solve by asking lots of questions instead of giving answers.**

   "What could you do about that?"

   "So, what will you do?" "What have you tried?"

   "How could you handle that differently?" "How could you approach the problem in a different way?"

   "What have you done in the past when you felt stuck like this?"

   "Why do you think she acted that way?"

"Is there anything you could commit to do differently that might make a difference?"

"You might want to take a break, calm down, & then come back and try again." "Be careful what you are saying to yourself, i.e. I can't do this!" Stop rescuing them! If there is a conflict at school with a teacher, help arrange a meeting between your child and the teacher, perhaps sit in the back of the room with tape over your mouth and support your child with your loving presence. Let them express their feelings and what they want. Allow the teacher and your child to work it out. This goes for issues with coaches as well.

Kids I've counseled who have made such an encounter happen have felt so empowered and proud of themselves. It gives them confidence that they can advocate for themselves with any future conflicts that will arise in their lives.

3. **Teach kids to handle their own conflicts with siblings and friends.** Teach them some conflict resolution skills at home when they are fighting with a sibling, then slowly back out of the job of being the judge, juror and executioner every time kids quarrel. When they come home upset by a conflict with friends, listen, ask questions, and help them brainstorm their own ideas about how to handle things. Then, throw them back out there. DO NOT rush up to school, confront the friend or call their friend's parents. I've seen it happen so many times where kids end up handling their issues, but their parents are still holding onto the hot potato that was their child's emotions and can't let go of it.

4. **Say NO!** Don't give in to their pestering, no matter how relentless they are. Set boundaries with your child's input about the number of activities they can be involved in or any purchases they want. (See Family Meetings, Chapter 9). Give kids an

allowance so that when they start on you about buying a toy at the store, you can calmly look them in the eye and say, "I'm not willing to buy it, but you can use your allowance money and get it if you want." That's a great way to teach kids the value of things and to delay gratification by learning to save their money in order to buy things. Kids learn tons about budgeting and saving. See Chapter 12 for more on allowances.

5. **Let your kids be frustrated, unhappy and suffer.** It's okay, really. It becomes great motivation to do things differently and learn from your choices and decisions. It allows kids to experience the consequences of their actions. Life is full of ups and downs for all of us; why should we rob them of the full ride? One of my favorite quotes says "Kids who don't have nightmares don't have dreams." I believe that's true.

    Kids also learn from adverse experiences that it's not what happens to you that's most important, it's what you do about it that matters. Overcoming obstacles and rising above challenges teaches kids to persevere and to be resilient—invaluable tools out in the real world. Grit and resilience are not gifts that we can give them; they have to be earned.

6. **Investment.** Kids need to be more invested in things, vs. just being given everything.

    A rottweiler, a chihuahua, and a tabby cat transitioned to the afterlife and were seated before the throne of God. God looked at each of them and asked, "What do you believe?" The rottweiler went first. "I believe in training, hard work, loyalty, unconditional love, and the protection of mankind." "Very good", said God, come sit next to me." The Chihuahua said, "Me too, me too. I believe in all of those things and in always being the best friend ever." "Then you shall join me as well", said God. "Tell me cat, what do you believe?" The cat yawned and replied, "I believe you are seated in my chair."

That is one entitled cat! When you've invested yourself in something through hard work, paying for it or helping to create it, you tend to care about it more, take better care of it and have more pride in it.

I met a successful businessman I'll call Henry several years ago who related a great story about getting your kids invested. His 16-year-old son Johnny wanted to go on a school trip to DC that cost $2500. Henry said he'd pay half if his son earned the other half. His son asked how he could earn $1250. Henry told his son, "I'll pay you $50 a week to cut our grass." The 1st time Johnny cut the grass he missed a lot of spots, so his dad took him out and showed him how to do it properly. Henry then told his son he'd deduct $10 for every spot he missed from then on. Lo and behold, Johnny did it right every time.

The evening before Johnny was ready to leave for his trip, he realized he was $50 short because he'd forgotten to figure in tax. Henry said, "Well then, I guess you can't go." Johnny was mortified and began to cry, but Dad persisted. So, Johnny went out to mow the lawn in the dark. Henry saw how hard his son was working, so he went out in the yard and held a flashlight as Johnny finished the grass. And I can tell you without a doubt that Johnny thoroughly enjoyed the trip!

This is a great example of the power of sweat equity. Whether it's sports camps, a new video game, or the latest name-brand shoes, have kids be more invested by earning them. There are more than enough opportunities for your children to make things happen for themselves.

7. **Kids need opportunities to work.** This can look like vacuuming, raking leaves, mowing the lawn, doing their own laundry, trimming trees, chopping and stacking firewood, sweeping out the garage, helping in the garden or building bookshelves for their rooms. Kids should pitch in with these kinds of tasks because they are part of the family vs. being paid to do chores.

We never tied allowance to chores in our home. You did chores because we were all expected to pitch in. We paid our daughter to babysit her youngest brother because she could have been down the street making money at a neighbor's. We also paid them to cut the grass because it's a two-hour ordeal. We felt that that was different because we'd have to pay another kid to do it if I couldn't. I want you to trust that there are some intrinsic rewards for helping out at home—pride in your work, a sense that we're all in this together. And you can make it fun too.

It's good to know how to work hard, to stay with a tough job. Plus, we forget that chopping wood and mowing the lawn at least initially allows kids to feel more grown and responsible; that's part of the intrinsic reward for a job well done. It's also another way to delay gratification because sometimes you can't go play ball on a Saturday morning until you cut the grass or do some other tasks.

Some parents don't give kids chores because they're worried that they are already stressed out and overwhelmed with all of their activities and school work. I don't buy that reasoning. Kids need to learn to balance their school work, activities, social life, family time and chores. You are preparing them for when they go off to college, get their first job, get married and have kids. All of us have to balance work, play and family time. Don't feel sorry for them, empower them. And if they truly are overwhelmed, then maybe it's time to take a good hard look at the number of commitments they've taken on and start doing some prioritizing and pruning.

8. **Walk your talk.** Finally, our modeling is perhaps our greatest teaching tool. They are watching how we live our lives, balance our lives, take or not take responsibility, save and budget and delay gratification, deal with materialism, enjoy or hate our work, and pull our weight at home.

One of Gandhi's famous quotes is, "Be the change you are trying to create." Make sure you are living and modeling the type of life and character you want your kids to emulate. Lots of parents today are distracted, too busy, out-of-balance and too dependent on externals to fill themselves up. Lots of adults are excessively into their "toys" and buying things.

Kids will always reflect the adult world around them, including parents, teachers, athletes, presidents and the culture at large. You have the most control over yourself and your behavior, so focus on that. And trust that if you don't overindulge your kids at home and if you model a healthy life, kids will get it no matter what their culture throws at them.

Chapter 4

The Goodwill Account

The absolute most important factor in keeping your family grounded is the state of the relationships in your home, i.e., how much goodwill is there in your relationships. By goodwill account (GWA), I mean, how much care and support are there between you and your kids? Between you and your spouse? Between siblings? The goodwill account provides the foundation from which everything flows in your family.

If your account with your children is full because you have been making regular "deposits," then your kids will feel close, safe, respected, heard, understood, trusted and trusting, powerful, accepted and loved. If the account is low because you have been making a lot of "withdrawals," then the relationship feels tense, distant, unsafe and disrespectful. In this situation, kids feel disrespected, angry, distant, not heard, unable to voice their concerns, overpowered, not important and unloved.

In this chapter, I will lay out the benefits of a full goodwill account and then give examples of withdrawals and deposits. Making a conscious, everyday effort to make deposits and keep the goodwill account full is the best preventative medicine for avoiding power struggles, anger and distance in your home, as well as ensuring that everyone feels grounded and connected. It's also what will best ensure that you remain an influence in your children's lives.

If a Goodwill Account is Full, Children and Parents are More Willing to:

- Be more open and transparent

- Listen to each other
- Be willing to sit down and have honest, heart-to-heart conversations about important matters
- Hear the other person's perspective or point of view
- Cooperate
- Pitch in when things need to be done
- Be more flexible
- Apologize when they were wrong
- Trust each other
- Be held accountable
- Express their feelings honestly and directly to the person involved
- Tell the truth
- Own up to and take responsibility for their mistakes and actions
- Sit down together and create win-win agreements
- Show their love and affection for each other
- Encourage and support each other

And by the way, this principle holds true for all relationships. When you see adults locked in bitter power struggles, i.e., spouses, business associates, employees or countries, the main culprit will be a low goodwill account. If there is little or no goodwill between two sides, it is next to impossible to negotiate in good faith or to sincerely listen to the other person's point of view.

Let's move on to some specific examples of how you can make deposits into your goodwill account with your children.

Goodwill Account Deposits

Respect

All kids need to feel respected by their parents. This is especially true during adolescence when teens are very sensitive to being disrespected by adults. And it is particularly important for kids who have an intense temperament that causes them to be very concerned with justice, fairness and respect. These strong-minded and independent-minded kids are very sensitive to being disparaged, and they will go to great lengths to demand respect. I've counseled hundreds of kids who are willing to be grounded, suspended, punished or fail in order to stand up to disrespectful and overpowering adults.

Respect can look like a lot of things, including not judging them or their friends by their external appearance, seeing things from their point of view, not yelling at them, and using their ideas in agreements (see Family Meetings, chapter 9). Respect looks like honoring a child's temperament and developmental level.

When our son John was four years old, we would take him to church with books, coloring books and crayons in tow. He would be fine for about 15-20 minutes sitting quietly in a place not the least bit designed for his needs. When we noticed his voice getting a bit louder and he was starting to drop things "accidentally" under the pew, I would walk him outside for five to ten minutes where we would look at the leaves, throw rocks, and talk out loud. After he blew off a little steam, we would head back into the church, where he could handle the last 20 minutes. By respecting his need for a break and handling it before he would lose it, we avoided a power struggle and a scene. In the process, we made a deposit into the goodwill account.

Kids feel respected when you get on their level when talking with them and use a regular voice vs. talking down to them. Respect means treating kids with the same respect you would show your best friend. You'd allow your best friend to say "no" to you, wouldn't you? You'd follow through on your agreements and promises and also hold them accountable to their agreements with you. You wouldn't have double standards with your best friend, yet we do it all the time with kids. "There is no yelling in this house!" we scream. Another example would be lecturing them about not drinking alcohol, especially not drinking and driving, and then getting behind the wheel after having a few beers or a glass of wine and driving the family home from a restaurant. Double standards smack of disrespect to kids.

Respect also looks like asking their permission before you give advice or feedback. That could look something like this:

Dad: *"Can I give you a suggestion about that?"*

Son: *"I guess."*

Dad: *"Are you sure it's okay?"*

Son: *"Yeah, I want to hear what you think."*

Then and only then would I give advice. That kind of respect feels great to kids and allows them to better hear you.

Listening

Being a good listener is a great way to make a deposit into the goodwill account. It needs to be the kind of listening where you get out of yourself and put yourself in your child's shoes in order to see an issue from their perspective. Kids feel like you really care about what they are saying and, therefore, you really care about them. I'll discuss this skill in great detail in chapter 5.

Special dates

One-on-one time in any way, shape or form is another important deposit. Kids feel special, important, close and loved. I recommend outside the house because there are fewer distractions, i.e., siblings with needs, phones, and T.V. Give your undivided attention to your "date."

It's nice to develop some special rituals with each of your kids. My daughter Kelly and I used to go to a used bookstore and hang out as we both loved to read. I always took my son TJ to breakfast at Bob Evans Restaurant before school. I'd order a decaf coffee; he'd order hot chocolate and we'd ask for an extra bowl of whipped cream. We'd play tic-tac-toe or Hangman until our food arrived. My son John and I regularly played basketball on our court. We made up our own versions of one on one with our own rules.

These special times don't have to be about spending money. It can be hiking down to the creek and skipping rocks like John and I used to do. Oftentimes, it is the more inexpensive, thoughtful, spontaneous times that create the most fun and bonding. And, it is during these moments when we are free from all of the distractions of home and work that we have some of our best discussions.

One of my favorite "date" experiences was taking my daughter Kelly on a weekend trip to Chicago for her 16th birthday. Every part of the trip was memorable. Even the flight and taxi rides were exciting for her. I remember taking her to a deep dish pizza place, where patrons could write on the walls, and looking for my signature I'd placed there while I was in college. Kelly loves singing and dancing, and she was thrilled we got to see the play "Ragtime." She was so cute the way she lined up her shampoo, conditioner and lotions in the hotel bathroom.

On the airplane to Chicago, I told her that one of the reasons I wanted this trip for the two of us was to show her by my example how a boy/man should treat her and that she should never settle for anything less. I count that trip as a major deposit into our goodwill account.

Perhaps my favorite way to spend one-on-one time when my kids were growing up was tuck-in time. I'd read a chapter from an old classic book like Robinson Caruso or Rebecca of Sunnybrook Farm to Kelly. I'd pull the covers over me and my sons and pretend we were in a tent camping out. We'd make up stories about bears or other jungle animals. At our summer camps, my wife Anne and I will go together to each cabin and tuck the campers in. That includes girls from grade school through high school. I can tell you with 100% certainty that kids are NEVER too old to be tucked in. Create your own bedtime rituals with each of your children. By the way, tuck-in times with the lights turned out are often the times when kids and teens are the most open for those heart-to-heart conversations. Don't skimp on these precious times.

Giving more power, say-so and control.

On the 1st day of school, a first grader handed her teacher a note from her mom. The note read: "The opinions expressed by this child are not necessarily those of her parents."

All kids want to have a voice, to be heard. All kids want a sense of control over their lives. To know that what they have to say matters, to have input into the rules and agreements they have to live by and to be part of the solution and agreement-making process. Kids who feel respected and empowered don't need to engage their parents in power struggles or rebel to gain a sense of control. This is especially true for kids who are powerful, independent-minded, and intense, like the first grader in the story above. Listen in to this dinner table conversation with a power-hungry kid:

6YO: "Can I eat a cookie?" Parent: "Finish your dinner first." 6YO: "My stomach is full except for a circle-shaped space."

The following are some concrete examples of ways to give kids more power at home in appropriate ways. For further information on this topic, see my previous book, *Food Fights and Bedtime Battles: A Working Parent's Guide to Negotiating Daily Power Struggles.*

1. Give choices. Let kids tell you what they want or need in order to create win-win solutions with them. For young children, it may be choices about what shirt to wear or what they want for breakfast. For a teenager, it might be about weighing options about a difficult decision or allowing them to choose to deal with a friendship issue in ways that you might think aren't the best.

Being able to make one's own choices gives anyone at any age a sense of empowerment.

2. Let them make decisions. There are tons of opportunities to let kids make decisions and then experience the consequences of their choices. If they make a good decision, they gain confidence in their ability to take care of themselves. If the decision turns out bad, they can learn something about themselves and grow wiser and stronger from the experience.

There are decisions about whether or not to join a soccer team, who to invite for a birthday party, how to handle conflicts with friends, what classes to take this semester, and what college you want to attend. Parents can be supportive by being a sounding board or by giving feedback, but only if the child asks for it. Unsolicited advice and problem-solving feel more like lecturing and non-listening and, therefore, are experienced as a withdrawal from the goodwill account.

3. Ask their opinion. This makes kids feel important, respected and noticed.

4. Let them say "no" to you. It is important and empowering for kids to be able to set boundaries at home. I'm obviously not talking about kids saying no to previously discussed agreements. But just as there are hundreds of opportunities for kids to learn to share and to give, there are also hundreds of opportunities for kids to practice saying "no" and setting limits, which is equally important for a healthy well-being.

I remember one time asking my then four-year-old son, John, if I could have a piece of his candy, and he said, "No." Although my immediate internal response was to feel indignant, angry and resentful (Who do you think earned the money for that candy, went to the store and bought it, by God?!), I calmly (I think) said, "Okay," and walked away. Just a few short minutes later, John walked up and offered me a piece of his candy. I think his initial "no" was just his way of testing whether or not his boundary would be respected. When it was, it created the space for him to choose to share with me vs. it being a "should" or "have to."

Also, if you want your kids, now and as adults, to be grounded, happy and emotionally healthy people, it's imperative that they can balance giving and receiving and being of service with saying no in order to take care of themselves. Being able to practice setting boundaries at home is empowering and it's a great deposit.

5. Give them greater responsibilities. It's very empowering to know from real experience that you can take on a job or task and see it through to completion. It is empowering to show that you are mature enough to be able to take care of your schoolwork and then totally own the results. You are preparing kids for when they leave the nest whenever you allow them to balance schoolwork, home chores, extracurricular activities and friend time.

My three kids all started doing their own laundry when they were in about 5th grade. The fun and novelty of the buttons and controls quickly wore off. But it turned into an internal pride. They felt proud and empowered that they could add doing their own laundry to an ever-increasing list of ways that they were able to take care of themselves. It's an intrinsic reward that can never be matched by being paid for it or praised for it.

6. Give kids more say-so in-home agreements. I will discuss this area in detail in the Family Meetings chapter (chapter 9).

7. Give kids more places to stretch themselves. See chapter 11 on giving kids opportunities to grow and more freedom.

8. Give kids more opportunities to be valuable. Parents of intense, strong-minded, power-hungry kids will always tell me that their kids are the most happy and grounded when they are being helpful or valuable. All kids love to make a difference. They love helping out at home, knowing that their contributions, no matter how small, are important and appreciated. Their contributions matter and so they matter.

When our son, T.J., was about 10 years old, he kept pestering me about wanting to cut the grass. Fearing the worst, I allowed him to cut the last few strips every week with me at his side, ever vigilant. One weekend, Anne's parents watched our kids at our house while we were out of town. When we pulled into the driveway on our return, there was my father-in-law sitting on a lawn chair sipping a glass of iced tea, watching T.J. cut the front yard! My initial shock was quickly tempered when I saw the look on T.J.'s face as he grunted and pushed that too-big-for-him mower. It was priceless. He was so happy and so proud of himself! He felt 10 feet tall and like a valuable "older" kid.

I saw an eight-year-old girl in my counseling practice once whose parents described her as an out-of-control, angry kid. Gabby engaged her parents in power struggles about everything, causing her parents to tip-toe around her for fear of setting her off. Interestingly, she was a perfect angel at school. When I talked to her alone, I remarked about the Girl Scout sash she was wearing. I told her a neighbor girl had just sold us cookies and had told me she had sold the most boxes in her troop, 100. Gabby told me she had sold the most boxes in her troop too, 185. Then she looked me in the eyes and stated proudly, "I love sales!" Powerful kids love to be valuable.

Remember that there are intrinsic rewards for being valuable and of service. It feels good on the inside to be helpful to someone—to know you made a difference. There is a sense of knowing you did the right thing.

These intrinsic rewards are the basis for self-motivation and are so much more important and fulfilling than external ones. So, don't pay your kids for chores or for pitching in around the house. Don't go overboard with too much praise. The external incentives distract kids from feeling the joys received from giving of one's self.

9. Let kids teach you things. Kids love to teach their parents new things. It allows them to feel more grown-up and more important. In those moments, they feel like they are on an even plane with their parents. It's very empowering for kids.

And this is true whether you're talking about a preschooler teaching you a nursery rhyme, a grade-schooler teaching you a card game they learned at camp, a middle schooler teaching you the latest dance steps, or a high schooler teaching you about what music is cool today and what's not. The fact that you listen, take them seriously and allow them to become the teacher while you become the student is a powerful message to them and a great goodwill account deposit.

10. Apologize when you are wrong. If you make a mistake or if you are wrong about something, make it a habit to own up to it and apologize. This is a very powerful deposit and it conveys a lot of respect for the other person.

I remember when our son, TJ, was about four or five years old, I spanked him for the first and last time. He was dragging his feet in getting ready for church one Sunday morning. He had a large container of crayons under his arm. I asked him to just take a few crayons in a sandwich bag, and he refused. When I came back a few minutes later, he again refused to take the big crayon box, throwing them down and yelling something at me. I just lost it, and as he ran by me, I popped his rear end, and he yelled again and ran upstairs to his room, with me in pursuit. Halfway up the stairs, I caught myself. I stopped and took a moment to cool off. When I went into his room, he was lying face down on his bed, crying, which made me feel even worse. I sat beside him and rubbed his back for a moment, apologizing about ten times for spanking him. He turned and *said to me, 'That's not the worst part; I was so shocked and scared running up the stairs that I peed my pants!" Well, he might as well have stuck a dagger in my heart. I could not have felt worse. He changed clothes, we drove to church, and as we were entering the building, I stopped and asked him to take a walk with me. We went over to the swing set, swung for a moment, and then I apologized again, telling him how bad I felt. I told him that I remembered my parents yelling at us as kids and being spanked and how I had sworn to myself that I would never do that to my kids. I committed to him that it would never happen again, a promise I kept for the rest of his childhood. I think I turned a withdrawal into a deposit with my apology.*

Connection

Imagine you are at a concert when you suddenly remember you forgot to turn the stove off. You become anxious about the stove, but you don't want to leave the theater—but you can't enjoy the music. This is an image of how most people live today: busy, distracted, disconnected, anxious, never present and not enjoying and savoring the moments.

Although this deposit seems obvious, in this hustle and bustle, busy world of ours, many kids feel disconnected. There are more parents working longer hours, more moms working full time, more single-parent households, more parents working from home, and don't forget all of our precious devices. And this can add up to parents who are tired, distracted, empty, crabby and impatient.

It's a huge withdrawal from the goodwill account when kids are with parents who aren't really there—who are at home but still in their work mode, distracted by job problems, emails and phone calls. It's also a withdrawal when you never have time as a family to sit down together for meals, play together outside after school, play board games after dinner and relax with each other during downtime. Those times are when kids feel most connected to their parents. One positive I heard from kids during the global pandemic was that with everyone home, there was more time for meals together and board games in the evenings.

The reunion time after school or when parents get home from work is a vital reconnecting time for children. I encourage parents to drop everything when they get home, put on some play clothes, and spend some uninterrupted time with their kids. Play tag, kick soccer balls, play loud music and dance, or curl up on a chair with them and read books or talk about their day. In some way, reconnect with each other.

This special time together gives everyone a chance to let go of their day and get back into home and family mode. Kids feel loved and secure, and this sets a warm tone for the rest of the evening. This 20-30 minute ritual pays huge dividends for all and is such an important deposit.

For many families, their after-work time ends up as a withdrawal. That's because kids feel they are rushed out of daycare by parents who are tired and impatient. When they get home, parents quickly become distracted with mail, emails, the evening news, making dinner and putting a load in the wash. As a result, kids feel disconnected and not important. A lot of the subsequent mischief in the evening (i.e., tantrums, power struggles, whining, arguing and sibling rivalry) is a direct result of kids feeling this way.

Make sure that everyone has a healthy late afternoon snack with some protein in it to hold them over so when you get home, they aren't hungry and crabby. Decide when you come home from work that nothing is more important than reconnecting with your kids. Mail, bills, laundry and dinner can wait a while. First things first. Play, have fun, snuggle, listen and laugh. Most important: reconnect.

One dad I met at a conference recalled how when he used to come home from work, his young children would excitedly rush up and give him hugs. But he got in the habit of walking into the house still finishing up phone calls. Sadly, he noticed that they stopped greeting him at the door. So, he made a commitment to himself that if he wasn't through with work calls, he'd sit in his car in the driveway until he was finished and then enter the house. Fortunately, his kids noticed and resumed greeting him at the door. He's never forgotten his pledge.

Goodwill Account Withdrawals

There are also things we do as parents that are withdrawals from our goodwill account with our kids. They are the opposites of deposits, i.e., being disrespectful, not listening, invalidating kids' feelings, not having time to be with them (especially special one-on-one time), being distracted when we are with them, being controlling and overpowering, not appreciating kids and their contributions, doing too much for them and not giving them chances to be valuable; yelling and spanking, and not apologizing when you are wrong.

These withdrawals leave kids feeling unloved, distant, overpowered, misunderstood, disrespected, not important, unsafe and lonely. If the goodwill account becomes low or empty because of frequent withdrawals, kids become less cooperative and less willing to sit down with parents and talk things through. It's impossible to create good win-win agreements when there is no "goodwill" in the relationship. And so parents and kids can stay stuck in a vicious cycle of feeling hurt and hurting back.

The solution? Start reestablishing the relationship by making deposits into the goodwill account. Be willing to make deposits tenfold, even if nothing comes back to you for a while. Hold off on agreements until the goodwill account fills up to the point where both sides are willing to listen and cooperate.

Prevention is always the best medicine for relationships. So, if you and your family are flying by the seat of your pants, put making deposits into the goodwill account at the top of your to-do list. Everything in your home will flow from the state of your relationships.

The other major benefit of a full goodwill account is that it can sustain families through tough times. All families go through stressful times when parents aren't as available to their children: i.e., the birth of a sibling, moves, illness, divorce, job loss or changes, tough stages with kids (like the teenage years), deaths, other stressful life transitions (menopause, aging or ill grandparents, kids transitioning to grade school, middle school, high school and college). These challenges can tear some families apart. But if your goodwill account is full, and kids feel very close to and loved by their parents, it's easier to get them through a period where parents might be distracted and less emotionally available. You will have lines of communication open for kids to express their feelings and ask for what they want and need. They trust your love and commitment to them. Everyone is more open to give and receive love and support. A full GWA can make all the difference in the world when times are tough.

I'll leave you with a touching poem:

What shall you give to one small boy, a glamorous game, a tinseled toy? A Boy Scout knife, a puzzle pack? A train that runs on some curving track. A picture book, a real live pet? No, there's plenty of time for such things yet.

Give him a day for his very own, just one small boy and his dad alone. A walk in the woods, a romp in the park, a fishing trip from dawn to dark. Give him the gift that only you can, the companionship of his old man. Games are outgrown and toys will decay, but he'll never forget if you give him a day.

Chapter 5

Listening

12-year-old Natalia had been venting to her dad about some major drama with her best friend when she suddenly stopped, looked her dad in the eye, and said, "You weren't listening to a word I said, were you?" Her dad responded, "That's a weird way to start a conversation."

Ugh! I bet a few of you reading this can relate to Natalia and her dad. So many of the girls I work with as a counselor and at my retreats and camps complain that their parents don't listen to them, leaving them feeling unimportant, misunderstood and unloved. Some of the most common culprits that keep us from being present listeners are busyness, external and internal distractions and multitasking. In addition, many parents grew up in an era where the parenting mantra was "kids should be seen and not heard." So, many parents never learned good listening skills growing up. This is one of the main reasons that marriages fall apart.

Being a good listener is a great way to make a deposit into the goodwill account. It needs to be the kind of listening where you get out of yourself and put yourself in your child's shoes in order to see an issue from their point of view. Kids feel like you really care about what they are saying and, therefore, you really care about them.

Two men were walking around New York City. One, a farmer visiting from Iowa, suddenly stopped in his tracks and said, "Listen, I hear a cricket." His friend told him he was crazy; there weren't any crickets in NYC, and if there were, he would never hear it over all the city noise. The farmer got quiet, bent down under a bush and found it. The New Yorker couldn't believe it. "You've got amazing hearing." The farmer responded, "No, it's just a matter of what you've been conditioned to listen for. I'll show you." He threw a handful of coins on the sidewalk, and immediately every head turned. *"See, you hear what you want to hear; it's a matter of what you're listening for."*

Being a good listener also entails knowing how to **mirror.** This involves listening to what your child has to say and then repeating back in your own words what you heard them say, i.e., paraphrasing.

Let me offer you an example of how mirroring would sound:

Natalia: *"My two best friends were mean to me today. When I asked to play with them at recess, they just turned their backs on me and walked away."*

Dad: *"So what I heard you say is that your two best friends didn't let you play with them today at recess. Did I get that right?"*

Natalia then can say that yes, Dad did hear her correctly, or if he missed something important, she can repeat it.

Natalia: *"Yeah, you heard me right. It made me so mad, but I just acted like it was no big deal. But it was."*

Dad*: So, it sounds like you got really angry when they excluded you, but you tried to act like it didn't bother you. Did I get that right?"*

Natalia continues sharing about her issue until she feels like her dad fully understands.

When a parent mirrors back what a child is trying to communicate, kids feel heard and cared about. They feel like their parents really understand them and that's a huge deposit for the GWA.

The next level of listening could then involve validating your child's feelings and positions.

Dad: *"You make sense to me because I know how much those friends mean to you, especially after your best friend from last year moved away. I imagine it hurt and might make you worry that you could be losing these friends too."*

Validating her feelings is a way of saying, *"I'm not you, but if I were you and had experienced what you experienced, it makes sense why you might feel that way."* You aren't saying you agree with them. You're just saying, *"If I were you and in your shoes, I might feel the same way; it's okay to feel whatever you are feeling; I understand."*

Once Natalia feels fully heard, then they could switch to problem-solving. But it's best if Dad first asks if she wants a suggestion.

Dad: *"Do you want me just to listen this time, or are you open to a suggestion?"*

Many times kids (and spouses) just want to be heard and validated. If Natalia says she'd like a suggestion, I'd ask again if she wants feedback. *"Are you sure you want some feedback?"* Then, if she says yes, I'd go on to problem-solving or perhaps give her another way of looking at the situation.

If Natalia had been sharing about something her dad had done that was bothering her, after she felt heard, he could ask her to listen to his side of the story. Dad would share his thoughts, and Natalia would mirror him until he felt fully heard.

Once both sides felt heard and validated, then they could take some time to find a solution that works for both of them. Win-win solutions only emerge when both sides are invested in hearing and respecting the other person's ideas, perspectives and needs. I'll discuss this more in the chapter on family meetings.

Once they've reached a solution that works for both of them, they could finish off the conversation by stating what the other person can count on them for going forward. *"You can count on me to put my phone away when we are playing board games so that you have my full attention."*

Think back to when you were a kid or teenager growing up. What was the thing your parents never understood about you that you always wished they would have? All of us have answers to that question. And it probably still hurts that some important part of you wasn't recognized, understood or validated. With this in mind, do your best to prevent that with your kids by making lots of listening, validating and understanding deposits into your children's goodwill accounts.

The following are common mistakes parents make when listening to their kids:

Be fully present. When parents are distracted and not fully engaged, kids feel unimportant, unloved, unheard, angry and not understood. A common reason most people struggle with listening, even when they have the intention of doing so, is that they fail to provide their undivided attention. Distractions, stress, worries and multitasking all interfere with high-quality listening. Some distractions are external, like checking your phone or watching a football game as you listen. Some are internal, like bringing home stress and worries from work that you can't shut off. *A dad told me once that during the holidays one year, he showed his wife and kids some old movies of them and their events growing up. He was taken aback when he realized that even though he had been the cameraman taking the videos, he had no recollection of these memories. He had been so wrapped up in starting a new business that he was never fully present during those years. That's an example of an internal distraction.*

So, in those moments when your child wants you to listen to them, drop everything and give them your full attention. It may require you to put your phone on silent mode or, better yet, put it in another room so you aren't tempted to glance at it. Kids deserve your full, undivided attention so that they know they are loved and important.

Stop giving me advice. Dads, listen up! Most kids just want to be heard when they are sharing their story or their emotions. They want to know that you see them, hear them, understand them and are on their side. My friend Dave describes this as being on team Chris (his son). It can be as simple as saying, "That really sucks." When parents quickly try to go into "fixit" mode, kids usually shut down because they are not there for advice; they just want to be heard. When kids, especially teens, share with their parents, they are often looking for a reality check, i.e., am I crazy for feeling this way? Being heard, giving them a hug or giving a little reassurance is more than enough. I feel like this is particularly hard for dads, as our brains are wired to fix problems. Learn to catch yourself and just listen. Practice with your spouse.

Don't make it about you. Girls tell me all the time that often, as they are sharing something emotional or intense, their mom turns their feelings back onto them. "You think you're stressed! What about all of the things I do around here and also work a full-time job!" This shuts down their daughter's sharing and makes the conversation about mom. Kids learn to believe that their feelings don't matter and that they need to take care of their mom's issues. I counsel so many girls who have come to believe that their feelings and needs are less important or, worse yet, that they shouldn't even have needs. Many of you moms reading this book right now are probably nodding your heads because part of our culture's good girl conditioning leads girls to believe just that.

Stop putting your crap into my story! Our children's emotions and experiences have the ability to trigger old feelings and unresolved issues from our past. This can result in us bringing excessive intensity and emotion to our child's experience. For example, I worked with a dad, Jeff, one time who was overreacting to his older son being too rough with his younger brother. Before the older boy could tell his dad his side of the story, Jeff exploded with anger at his eldest before he could catch himself. He shared with his sons and me that he, too, had an older brother who took out his anger on him, and he felt bullied his entire childhood. He still carried a lot of anger and frustration at his parents for not stepping in and protecting him. Jeff vowed to himself that when he had kids, he would make sure they all felt safe and protected. That's a healthy intention, but unfortunately, the older son's rough play sparked old feelings of anger and helplessness that erupted in the present day. Having that awareness helped Jeff to not bring the old story and feelings from his past into his son's relationship where it did not belong. Kids have enough to deal with due to their own emotions and don't have the ability to handle their own if we overwhelm them with our stories and emotions.

Stop playing hot potato with my emotions! Many times, when a girl brings home stories about being left out or teased by her best friend, it comes out as intense venting. Afterward, she feels relieved and lighter for having let go of her emotions, but guess who oftentimes is left holding onto them? You got it, her parent. She'll go to school the next day, and the girls make up, but her mom is still holding onto negative feelings about her daughter's friend. If you're still holding onto the feelings, you will continue to judge the friend, make snarky comments about her or try to limit your daughter's time with her. Your daughter won't feel safe to share future stories with you because of the way you played hot potato the last time she shared. Parents need to learn not to take on their children's feelings. You can mirror, empathize and validate their feelings without joining them on their normal adolescent emotional roller coaster.

Stop hailing on me! I use a fabulous metaphor called the turtle and the hailstorm to demonstrate how to make it safe for teenagers to share more with their parents. Teenagers are the turtle, and their parents are the hailstorm. It's normal for teens to start wanting more privacy and space from their parents. They often don't want their mom and dad to be privy to their dating relationships or friend issues. That is represented by the turtle who pulls back some into her shell. Because said teen is not sharing quite as much and spending more time in her bedroom and out with friends, parents start to feel disconnected and unsure if she is alright. When she comes home from school in a tizzy and ignores her mom's 50 questions about "What's wrong?" and "Are you okay?" and marches straight up to her bedroom and slams the door, parents become even more worried. So, what do they do? They hail, i.e., they ask more questions, become more intrusive, and bring more intensity and worry to their questioning. This, of course, annoys the turtle teen to no end, and so she retreats further into her shell. This makes Mom and Dad even more worried…I think you can see the pattern now.

The way out of this struggle requires both parties to act differently. I encourage teens (turtles) to poke their heads out more and give their parents more information about how they are thinking about important matters like sex, drugs, their education, college plans, etc. It pays for them to be more transparent so that their folks don't feel so disconnected. Most times, they are more thoughtful and mature about issues than their parents are aware of, and this helps allay parental fears. The parent's responsibility is to stop hailing, i.e., stop over worrying and asking 50 questions, especially right when they walk in the door after school. Parents can learn to give their teenagers the space they need to work through a challenge. And parents can let them know that they are there if they want to bounce something off of them. If parents have a history of being good listeners, their turtle will be more likely to do so. When parents stop hailing, it's easier for turtles to stick their heads out of their shells. So both parent and child have a part in resolving this issue.

Respect my context! There is an insightful story that demonstrates this next mistake parents make with listening. *Elephants became popular in circuses in England in the 19th century. One circus owner bought an elephant to display to his crowds. After a few days, the elephant's personality changed, and it started charging towards kids who approached his cage. It also tried to kill his keeper, so the owner decided he needed to put it down. To try to make up for his losses, the owner decided to make it a public execution and charge money. A large crowd showed up for the performance, and right before his men shot the elephant, a small man wearing a brown derby walked through the crowd and asked for two minutes with the angry elephant to prove them wrong. The circus owner was worried about the liability of this, so the stranger signed a waiver. He removed his coat and hat and entered the cage as a hush fell over the crowd. The elephant reared at him but the man began to speak to him in a soft voice and in a strange language. The beast let out a pitiful cry and relaxed. The man stroked his trunk, and all aggression drained from it. The little man held the elephant's trunk and slowly led him around the cage. He then said goodbye to his new friend and left the cage. The owner was incredulous, but the stranger explained what had happened. "He's an Indian elephant, and none of you spoke his language; I'd advise you to get someone here who speaks his language. He's not angry, just homesick." With that, the man put on his coat and derby and left. The circus owner looked at the waiver, and saw it was signed by the famous author Rudyard Kipling.*

If you want your kids to come to you when they are hurting or need advice, you must learn the best context for each child that allows them to feel safe to do so. Some kids are fine with a face-to-face sit-down, but many, especially boys, are not. Those kids are often more comfortable with what people call side-by-side conversations. This could mean they are more open to talking while riding in the car with you, walking side-by-side, playing catch or sitting in the stands at a game. Some kids are more open and vulnerable when the lights are out, and you are sitting on their bed, tucking them in. Others share more clearly through writing you letters. The point is to discover what the best context is for each of your children that will allow you to open the door to their hearts.

Unrushed, focused time. The phrase *"take all the time you need"* is magical to children. When a parent sits down and gives their child their full attention anytime they have important things to tell them signals that what they have to say is important and, in turn, they are important. It means that there is nothing more important in the world right now than the child. "Take all the time you need" is a fabulous deposit for the goodwill account and the key to remaining an influence in their lives throughout their teen years and beyond.

Chapter 6

Time Together Inside

I see a lot of families play out the following scenario each night at home: see if you don't see yourself in here somewhere.

Everyone arrives home around 6 p.m., exhausted from their busy day. Mom picked up feisty four-year-old Danielle from daycare, where a major tantrum erupted because she wanted to play longer and her rushed mom didn't let her. So, mom crammed her into her car seat and drove off with one hundred decibels blaring from the back seat.

The next stop was after-school care, where seven-year-old Chris and ten-year-old Tyler were picked up. As soon as they drove away from school, the bickering started between the two boys. Mom nags, scolds and barks at them to stop, all to little avail. By the time they roll into the driveway, Mom's nerves are frayed. Once inside, all hell breaks loose.

Dad arrives to add his crabbiness to the mix. The kids get their way and have cookies before dinner just to shut them up. Dinner is somehow thrown together, and then most of the mealtime is spent redirecting poor table manners and arguing between the siblings.

After dinner, there is the obligatory hour of power struggles over homework and baths, with Mom and Dad ending up doing way too much homework, nagging and yelling. There are struggles over brushing teeth, baths and getting kids settled into their beds. It's now 8:30 p.m., the kids are continuing to push their bedtime and mom and dad have had it. Their parenting day ends with them yelling at their kids or laying with them until they fall asleep. It's now 9:30 p.m., and Mom and Dad sleepwalk through some final tasks before passing out at 10:30 p.m.

Notice there wasn't much time to play in there? Or hang out? Or relax? Or be together? Kids too often feel rushed, disconnected and stressed, and so do their parents. But it doesn't have to be this way. Really!

I saw a nine-year-old boy, Russ, recently in my practice who had a strained relationship with his father. His dad worked long hours, traveled a lot, and had very little energy for anyone when he came home every evening. He made it for dinner a few nights a week, and other nights he'd arrive at 8 or 9 p.m. Even when he was home, he was constantly distracted with his cell phone and work emails. He was distracted and stressed out a lot.

I had the dad listen to his son in my office and what he heard was interesting. Russ said that even when his dad did play floor hockey in the basement or played catch in the back yard it still wasn't fun. His dad was constantly checking his watch and cell phone, had set a very strict time limit on the game (I can only play for 15 minutes), and when the time was up he rushed off to his computer to do more work.

Russ told his dad that when he did that, he felt like his dad didn't care about him and that his work was more important than him. He also felt his dad didn't really want to play with him or enjoy it; he was only doing it because he had to and because Mom made him.

I think a lot of kids feel like Russ. In chapter 4, I gave suggestions about how to make regular deposits into the Goodwill Account. In chapter 9, I will discuss how family meetings can be a place where kids and parents can ask for and create more time together. In chapter 8, I'll be discussing the importance of creating family rituals and traditions together. And in chapter 7, I'll discuss ways to enjoy family time together in nature. In this chapter, I'll focus on some ways to enjoy time together inside your home.

First of all, remember that most people, kids and parents alike, need to transition from school to home or work to home. Some kids are over-stimulated and mentally exhausted when they arrive home after school. They might need 15-30 minutes of quiet alone time in their room to re-group and re-fuel. This would not entail TV, video games, or phone time because those things zone you out vs. re-fueling you. It could mean a short nap, listening to music, art, reading or building something. Or it could mean sitting on dad's lap and reading books or laying on the bed together, venting about their day. Many kids need to blow off steam by going outside and kicking soccer balls or jumping on the trampoline. The most beneficial breaks involve three aspects: moving, going outside and unplugging from technology.

The same goes for parents. Some parents stop at a workout place on the way home; for others, a long commute home with quieting music helps their transition. When you get home, change into play clothes and spend some focused time playing with your kids. Don't rush right into dinner or chores. Everyone needs to reconnect.

Remember, too, that a fun, interactive family dinner is a great way to be together. Talk about your day, have each person share their best and worst moments from the day (commonly called the high-low game or thorns and roses), and be sure to include everyone in the conversation. Go to my website at www.drtimjordan.com/products to find my **Dinner Dialogue Cards** to give you lots of examples of prompts you can share.

Cooking the meal and cleaning up can also be fun if everyone pitches in and you keep the mood light. At my weekend retreats, we cook all of our meals together with the campers doing a lot of the work. They crack eggs, make grilled cheese sandwiches, and we even make chocolate chip cookies from scratch. There is a rumor that we even allow a bit of cookie dough sampling. I get volunteers to help me clean up the dishes and they love it! We created some chants that we scream out as we put dishes into the sanitizer. We blare fun dance music to lighten the mood. It really is a blast and a lasting memory for the campers. Their parents don't believe it when we tell them how amazing their daughters were in cleaning up the meal messes.

The following are some examples of ways to spend special inside time with your kids instead of parking in front of the TV or computer screen.

Letter Writing

Writing thank you notes or letters to loved ones is becoming a lost art. Kids love to send pictures they've drawn or notes to grandparents, friends who moved away or pen pals.

I had an author, Mark Button, on our radio show once who talked about his book *The Letter Box*. One great idea I got from the book is for every family member to decorate a letter box for themselves (shoebox size). The box serves to store letters that siblings, parents, relatives or friends send to you that are to be opened at specific times. For instance, parents could write a letter to be opened on different life stages like birthdays or graduations.

I published a book a few years ago entitled *Letters From My Grandfather: Timeless Wisdom For a Life Worth Living*. In it, a girl got a surprise letter box from her beloved grandfather after his passing. There are letters for her to open on her 16th and 18th birthdays, high school and college graduations, her 1st day of college, her 21st birthday, etc. Each letter contained some wisdom for her that pertained to that life stage.

The letter box can also store your favorite notes and birthday cards from loved ones. Our kids each had such a letter box. We started a tradition at our summer camps years ago where parents secretly write their camper a love letter that we have them open and read on the last night of camp to prepare them for going back home. There are always many tears shed and lots of smiles. Our campers also get a love letter from their special camp counselor, and so our three kids all have many such keepsakes from all of their camp years. They even took them to college for reassurance during any times of self-doubt. And kids can write letters to relatives with the same intention. What a special tradition that would be for any family.

Scrapbooking

I describe Anne and my experience with this idea at a Mother-Daughter retreat in chapter 8. It could be a fun, never-ending project for the whole family in your home. Ask older relatives for pictures, and even better, have them tell your kids the story behind the pictures of their ancestors. Kids could make scrapbooks of their own lives with photos, drawings, concert tickets, etc.

Family Journal

Have the kids pick out a journal with you, then leave it out in a central place in your home. Anyone can write in it at any time. Encourage kids to write entries about how they are feeling about themselves, their relations with the family members, and their worries or desires. Or it can be a place to correspond in a safe way to another family member.

I kept a running journal of our family meetings for years. I wrote the cute, funny and poignant things that were shared and the topics that were important at the time in our family with the intention that someday it would be fun to read back through it as a family—to remind us of our journey together. A few years ago, I found that journal and we all read through it during the holidays when our now adult children were all home. It brought back so many memories and lots of laughs.

Games

Some of my most fun memories from our summer camps are the silly games we play in the evenings. This ranges from never-ending spicy Uno to Egyptian Rat Screw or Pictionary. When our good friends came over for our annual New Year's Eve get-together, we always played at least one game of Skip-Bo with all ten of us participating.

Our family went through phases of Mancala, spades, dominoes, and Monopoly. We often made up our own rules. My sons loved to snare me into long battles of "Risk." Card games, trivia games and Doctor Tangle have all been played out in our family room.

Reading

Visiting the library, bookstores and annual book fairs creates more than enough reading material. I loved sharing my old *Hardy Boys* books with my sons. My son John loved reading my old copies of *The Hobbit* and *Lord of the Rings* in middle school long before the movies came out. Some of my favorite memories from when our kids were young was reading to them at bedtime. And I tried to be sure it wasn't rushed time.

Making Movies

Most kids love to make movies. Now that our kids are adults with spouses and our grandkids, we can look back and roar with laughter at their home-made efforts; seeing Kelly and her friend cheerleading and dancing to "Ace of Base," John dancing like Michael Jackson at four years old, and watching TJ and his friends enacting a scene from a movie is priceless. Kids really get into the process of preparing, practicing, filming and editing.

Tuck-ins

One of my favorite times of the day and favorite memories. Again, this should be unhurried time. When you turn the lights out and sit on the edge of the bed or lay with your kids, they should feel like you have all the time in the world and that they have your full attention. This is the time when many kids are most open and vulnerable—when they will share things with you that they wouldn't earlier in the day. Rub their backs, massage their feet and listen and learn. I hope my kids' memories of those evenings are as warm as mine.

Movie Nights

I love watching movies, and so do my kids. We used to go to the video store on Friday evenings, and they'd pick out their favorite snacks to go along with a movie rental. We'd build a fire in the fireplace, get in our pajamas, watch the movie, eat our goodies and have a ball. My two sons and I, to this day, talk a lot in movie lines, which my wife still can't quite connect to. When our kids were young I'd show them old classics like Shirley Temple or Jerry Lewis movies. I can't get away with that anymore.

So, whether it's meals, games, books, scrapbooks, journals, dances, movie nights or tuck-ins, the intention was time together as a family. And it was time together that allowed a lot of conversation, laughs, memories and creativity. None of this happens much when you spend a lot of time plugged into home entertainment centers: TV, video games, or computers, iPads, and smartphones.

Be creative and listen to what is fun for your kids and make this kind of time a priority. If you don't, it won't happen very often. Take a good, hard, honest look at your family's schedule, and do some pruning if it's too cluttered with activities and busyness. It's easy and all too common today to get out of balance. Don't let that happen to your family.

Chapter 7

Time in Nature

Somehow, someway, we have lost some of the old traditional ways of connecting with our loved ones. Blame it on the Industrial Revolution or urbanization or technology, but the fact of the matter is that we as a culture have lost the ability to have fun and to do more with less. We have lost the ability to enjoy the slower, simpler pleasures of life. We have been conditioned to need quick sound bites of fun and immediate gratification. When our computers take five seconds to spit forth their information, we become impatient and frustrated. We need to be constantly entertained and stimulated at high-intensity levels. Because of this, we are missing out on a lot of vintage moments and experiences—moments of closeness and wonder. The best remedy for what ails us is spending time in nature with your family.

Despite your already overloaded schedule, you may realize you have more time than you first thought once you become involved in these activities. These are experiences that help our children learn the value and magic of watching things grow from a seed over weeks and months. Quiet moments that allow us to watch constellations slowly drift across the sky from season to season (or clouds from minute to minute) and that help us watch birds from the onset of nest-building through the egg stage to a mature bird. We help our children and ourselves notice and appreciate the passing of time, seasons and cycles of nature, to learn to relax and smell the roses (and plant some, too!). This chapter was one of my favorites to write.

There is something very grounding (pardon the pun) about spending time in nature that isn't experienced anywhere else.

There is something in the air, earth, water, stars, woods, etc., that gives us pause, relaxes us and refocuses us.

All of our greatest spiritual teachers from all religions have told us as much. Moses went up into the mountains and came back with the Ten Commandments. Moses spoke to God in the desert in the form of a burning bush. Paul was jolted with a life-changing experience while riding a horse. Jesus went out into the desert for forty days and forty nights to meditate, pray and become inspired for his teachings. On Jesus' final night, he went outside in the garden to pray. Buddha sat under a tree beside a river and became enlightened. When Gandhi became frustrated with the civil wars between his people, he went out into the countryside, simplified his life, took long walks and spun yarn. The prophet Muhammad included a holistic view of nature in his teachings.

Nature is the place to relax, get clear about questions you may have, get refocused, ground yourself, get refueled when you feel empty and experience awe.

Mary Pipher, author of *The Shelter of Each Other,* notes research that shows that the three things adults remember most fondly about growing up are family vacations, family dinners together, and family time in nature. Bring some of your own childhood family memories of time outdoors to life through stories and repeating these wonderful traditions in nature.

The following are some examples of how to spend time with your family in nature:

Walking

Just plain old-fashioned walking around the block is a great way to relax together after dinner or anytime. And don't let darkness or cold weather hold you back. Get off that stupid treadmill in your moldy basement and walk outside! Added benefits include walking off that dessert you just ate and meeting your neighbors.

Many kids, especially boys, who won't give much information with direct one-on-one questioning will start chattering away when you are strolling around the block. They feel safer to share when it's not such an intense, direct confrontation.

Many families today spend much of their downtime huddled in front of their home entertainment centers, thus never getting to know their neighbors. Most kids know more about the personal lives of celebrities and Oprah than they do about the people who live next door. It's sad when you think about it.

Most cities have parks with well-marked trails which are even more fun to explore. Make sure everyone has a good walking stick (finding them along the trail is half the fun). Take your time and explore every creek bed, climb over every log, swing on every vine, and make guesses about every animal track you discover. Younger kids love to collect treasures on nature walks so bring along a backpack. Don't rush through the woods because you will miss too many sights, sounds and adventures. I find it best to go at your child's speed and not rush them.

The retreat facility I use for our school year overnight camps has a river running through it. We always take kids on a hike and end up at the river. And these normally rushed, over-scheduled kids and teens have a blast! We let them wade out into the current, splash each other, teach kids to skip rocks and just play. So many kids rarely get the opportunity to have time in nature like that with no agenda or time restraints. Let me highlight that thought: no agenda, no competition, no prizes or trophies, no devices, no time restraints, no adult telling them what to do. Kids need that kind of unsupervised, undirected time.

We usually hike back to camp by walking up a creek bed. And by the time we reach the top, even the prissiest kid is knee-deep in water and mud, totally engrossed and having spontaneous fun in the moment. That's the key. Just being present in nature and in the moment.

When was the last time you and your kids took a nature hike where it was not only okay but encouraged to explore and get dirty? Where you had more than enough time to really explore your environment without having to check your watch every ten minutes because you were worried about missing a soccer game. Think about it.

Stargazing

One summer, when our kids were in grade school and middle school, the Jordan family, along with our friends and their three kids (six kids and four adults total), drove out to Colorado for a vacation. The second night was spent camping out in the mountains along a whitewater river on a gorgeous, clear evening. After dinner I invited all the children to come lay down on the rocks by the river to look for shooting stars. My suggestion was met with looks of disbelief and boredom, but I went anyway. A short time later, I was joined by the other parents. Gradually, one by one, the six children, ages 8-16, sauntered down to the river until all ten of us were lying on sleeping bags, stargazing. There's nothing quite like the night sky when you are up in the mountains. About every five minutes or so, they would see a shooting star. It was one of the most relaxing, peaceful, and fun times of the ten-day vacation. Everyone enjoyed a much richer show than anything they could have watched on a screen.

What better way to slow down and unwind at the end of a hectic day than to sit outside and try to find the Big Dipper, Orion or Pegasus? You do not have to be an astronomer to enjoy the night skies with your family. Go to the library or bookstore and pick up a book about constellations. Use an app like Skyview or Skymap to identify the different constellations and planets.

Because our earth and solar system are constantly moving, the skies look different at different times of the year.

Some of my favorite memories of our summer camp occur when we lay out a big tarp in the middle of a field, turn out all the camp lights and stargaze. There is something magical about looking up at the stars, trying to identify constellations and watching vigilantly for shooting stars. We talk, tell stories, joke around and connect in a very special way. There's something unique and special about being outside, in the dark, laying on your back on good old Mother Earth, and looking at the heavens. Many of our conversations become deep discussions about life, death and whatever else is on kids' minds.

I have several stars that remind me of certain kids or certain memories. A big group of us one night had some incredible discussions while stargazing on a hill at camp, and we decided that every time we saw the North Star we would remember that night. This was an example of savoring the moment. One of the stars of the big dipper reminds me of Meg, Sasha and Brittany because I had told them stories every night at camp one week. So, whenever they miss each other and camp, they just go outside, find that star and remember our fun and close times together.

Develop those kinds of moments and memories with your kids.

Campfires

Who doesn't enjoy a good campfire? Who doesn't love staring at the fire, roasting marshmallows, making s'mores, singing campfire songs and telling stories? Both little kids and big ones love to get a stick in their hands and poke and prod the wood and coals. I find boys especially become mesmerized by a campfire.

Even making the fire is an opportunity to connect with your kids. Take the time to patiently teach your kids about how to make a teepee or a log cabin campfire. Even gathering and cutting the wood is a chance to teach kids about nature and for them to feel valuable.

There was an eight-year-old named Charlie with cerebral palsy at our camp years ago who was very frustrated by his inability to play sports and get around as easily as his siblings and peers. The turning point in camp for him was our peaceful warrior night. One of our counselors, Louie, recognized Charlie's need to feel valuable so he took Charlie with him to make the campfire. When we brought the group down to the fire, there was Charlie grinning from ear-to-ear with black coal marks on his face and some scratches on his arms, right smack dab in front of a huge, glorious, blazing bonfire. He couldn't have been more pleased and proud of himself. He was a different kid the rest of the week. That's the power of nature and a campfire at its best!

Backyard fireplaces can be bought at your local hardware stores allowing you a legal campfire at home. I guarantee it will attract tons of neighborhood kids and adults alike. It's a great way to break the ice and meet people on your street.

And while you are enjoying the fire, why not create a storytelling tradition? Everyone, kids included, could recite their favorite scary story, family story or animal tale. Create a campfire tradition for the first and last days of summer, holidays, the last weekend before school starts and the first weekend after school ends to get everyone together. There's nothing quite like gathering family and friends around a campfire, whether on a mountaintop or in your backyard.

Bird Watching

This idea may sound a little square, but bird watching can become a great family tradition in nature.

I bought a bird feeder and then made two others many years ago and placed them in our yard in full view of our kitchen window and my upstairs office. The kids and I were fascinated by all of the different varieties of birds that visited our feeders. The variety of birds necessitated a trip to our library to look up these birds in bird books.

It's still very relaxing for me to sit in my office when I need a break and watch the birds below me. At the other end of the emotional spectrum, we had some pulse-racing exciting moments as well.

We watched on several occasions as nature unfolded before us. A hawk visited our yard occasionally and hunted the smaller birds. We watched in silence and awe as the hawk stalked the little birds, with the victims hiding in a nearby bush. And together, they played a hide-and-seek hunting game. It was fascinating to watch and much more exciting and real than anything on TV. One time we even watched some large black birds attacking the hawk as he flew off with one of their kind in his talons. Awesome!

Feeding these birds throughout the winter also allowed our family a sense of giving. Watching these birds, who build nearby nests, hatch from eggs was another gift from our bird feeders. And it was fun and relaxing to sit out on our deck and watch the different birds fly in and out. Have your kids help you build some feeders and put food in them. It's another way to make them feel valuable and important. There are lots of good books at the library/bookstore showing how to build different types of feeders for different types of birds in different climates as well as how and what to put in feeders to attract different varieties of birds. Check it out and enjoy!

Gardening

Most kids love to play in the dirt, so gardening is just a step up from that. Remember the joy your kids experienced in kindergarten when they brought home the seed in the famous Styrofoam cup and watched it grow into a plant? Recreate that feeling on a bigger scale with gardening together.

Think about how rushed we all feel today: go-go-go constantly, and then compare that with the slow, patient pace of gardening. The essence of gardening is patience, delayed gratification, persistence, hard work at the beginning with big rewards at the end, and a result that can be given away over and over again. There are lessons about weather, seasons, growth, life and death. It sounds a bit dramatic, but it's true. There's something very grounding about getting your hands in soil and messing around in it.

To make the experience most valuable for your kids, have them involved every step of the way. That includes buying the seeds or plants, preparing the soil, reading up a bit on when and where to plant, caring for different plants, harvesting flowers, vegetables and fruits, and preparing the soil in the fall for next spring.

My grandson Lou started helping me in my garden at age four. I let him dig the holes and plant the seeds in whatever pattern he wanted. He loved getting his hands in that dirt! Every time he came over to our house all summer long, the first place we'd go was down to the garden to check on the progress of his vegetables and flowers. I think this will be a memory he reminisces about fondly.

Having kids help with the watering, feeding and pruning is a great lesson in stick-to-itiveness. It's also very relaxing to water flowers and the garden in the evening. After dinner and before dark is a glorious time of the day to spend in your yard with your family. There is a certain peace and calm that you just don't feel at any other time of the day.

Planting trees is another grounding activity. My wife Anne's parents used to own a farm about two hours from St. Louis. When we moved into our house, we dug up some trees at the farm and replanted them in our own new yard. The two silver maples covered our front yard with shade, and the three white pines lined the back of our yard. Even though they sold the farm years ago, the five trees are a living monument to the memories of the fun times we all had at Grandma and Grandpa's farm.

I wish now that we'd had our kids stand in front of those trees every year on their birthdays with a sign showing the date, their age and their height. What a great way to measure growth over time!

One year, my son John, then nine years old, bought Anne a rose bush for Mother's Day. We planted it together for her on Mother's Day, and 25 years later, that rose bush is still cranking out beautiful salmon-colored flowers to decorate Anne's table. John was so proud of himself. It also sparked an interest in roses in yours truly. Our yard at one point contained 40 rose bushes, many of which were planted with the help of my seven-year-old nephew John, who is my godchild. Lots of people have received beautiful roses to take home as a result of my son and I's Mother's Day gift.

Animals

There are great places in all areas of the country to enjoy animal life indigenous to that area. In St. Louis, there is a wolf sanctuary, places to see buffalo, and a world-class zoo. There are places along the Mississippi River where you can go in the winter and see bald eagles that hibernate there every year. There is a butterfly house two miles from where I live where you can go and see all the different species of butterflies year-round.

Find these types of opportunities to be around animals. Kids love it, and it's yet another way to be out in nature together.

There are so many creative ways to spend time in nature together with your family: building forts and tree houses, climbing trees, sitting on a hillside and looking for pictures in the clouds, apple picking at farms in the fall, backpacking or camping out at state parks or even just in your own backyard. It will be time well spent and such a different feeling than if you'd been sitting indoors. More talking, more sharing, more laughing, more connecting, and more memories that will last a lifetime.

Chapter 8

Traditions and Rituals

Participating in family traditions and rituals, old and new, is another way to keep your family grounded. It's harder for a lot of families today because of how mobile our society has become. Going to college means you may end up marrying someone and moving to their hometown. Job changes cause many families to move away from home or even move many times while raising their kids. With grandparents, siblings, aunts and uncles living far away, it can be more of a challenge to keep old family traditions alive.

There are many important benefits resulting from family traditions. They are a way to connect kids to their past; it gives them history. And that history gives kids a sense of connectedness and security about who they are. When you go through all of the questioning about your identity during your teen years, it helps to know where you come from.

When I was growing up, I loved having relatives who would tell me stories about my parents when they were my age, when they were dating, just married and so on.

I still do. I love hearing stories about my deceased grandparents. And I love hearing stories about how much I look like my grandfather or how my son looks and carries himself like his great-uncle Tony's side of the family. Kids love stories that connect them to their past.

Anne and I ran a four-day mother-daughter retreat in Colorado several years ago. The girls were ten to thirteen years of age. We did all kinds of fun and intimate exercises with them about strengthening their communication skills and their relationships. On their evaluations, most of the girls said their favorite activity was the scrapbooking session.

We had told the moms ahead of time to bring old pictures of women in their daughter's family tree from both parent's sides. And we suggested they be able to tell stories about each of these women. The moms also brought pictures of themselves at different ages in their lives, including their daughter's present age, as well as pictures of the two of them together at different stages.

And so, while they put the pictures in the scrapbook, the moms told the girls stories about their relatives, including insights into these women's characters. The moms also told their daughters how they were like some of these ancestors in looks and in personality. The girls just soaked it all in. What a keepsake to keep adding to over the years.

Think about what family traditions meant the most to you growing up and figure out how to recreate these with your family today. If you can't recreate the actual experience, then get clear about what emotions are associated with the old tradition and start a new tradition that creates the same feelings within your family. Oftentimes, it's not the exact experience that's most important. What we really want is to recreate the good feelings that we associate with it: closeness, warmth, a sense of belonging and love.

My family has a tradition of a big family get-together meal on Christmas. It's always the same meal: beef broth soup, my mom's special salad mixed by hand in a couple of extra-large salad bowls, and then homemade ravioli with our famous family sauce. My grandparents and aunts and uncles used to roll out their own ravioli each year on a Sunday while all the grandchildren played together. These days, we buy them every year from the same Italian bakery in St. Louis. My kids always look forward to this delicious meal.

Anne's mom's side of the family has a different tradition, a family reunion meal, which has been going on for over 100 years. Anne's parents grew up in a small farming town a couple of hours south of St. Louis, and the big-city relatives used to rent a bus and drive down to the reunion together. These days, most of the relatives live in St. Louis, so it's held there.

The meal is always turkey and dressing and mashed potatoes. And the money needed to buy all the food is made from the annual fall apple butter cooking. Four generations of family members meet at someone's farm and cook apple butter all day long in huge copper kettles, with every generation pitching in. Young kids stir the pot, and the elderly taste the butter every so often and instruct everyone about what to add to make the perfect apple butter. When done, the apple butter is poured into pint and quart jars that are then sold (mostly to those present), and the money is used to create our Christmas meal.

Another Jordan staple at any get together is eye-of-the-round beef sandwiches. My dad, who passed away 30 years ago, had a special way to smoke it on the grill and then take it to the butcher to be sliced extra thin. I have shown my sons how to do it, and the tradition thus carries to the next generation. My son always felt close to his grandpa, so it's a special way to bring back his memory. He asked me once if anyone else knew how to prepare the eye-of-the-round like Grandpa did. I asked him "Have you ever seen it or had it anywhere else like this?" He smiled and said no. This sort of tradition can mean a lot to kids.

In my neighborhood growing up, we had several annual get-togethers. There was the all-neighborhood Fourth of July softball game at the nearby middle school field. There was the after-trick-or-treating hot chocolate party at the Potter's house on Halloween. And, there was the Christmas caroling to collect money for a charity and, of course, the get-together afterward. I cherish all of those memories.

I would also encourage all of you to start some new traditions with your own family. When our kids were young, I started buying white ceramic snow village buildings for our kids to paint.

I remember us all sitting at the kitchen table, painting and chatting away. The kids always painted a school and gave it to their teachers for a Christmas present. And we started displaying our artwork in our foyer.

We started out with a few buildings on a card table, but after many years, we had a large table filled with churches and schools and libraries and shops, along with cotton-snow and trees and carolers. It's still fun to look at the splotchy paint jobs from their kindergarten years, but the kids still put all of these treasures out proudly every year.

One Christmas, the Jordan get-together was at our house, with 34 people total. After dinner, we decided to go around the table and have everyone share one of their highlights from the past year. There were some uncomfortable groans and sarcastic comments at first, but it turned out to be a great experience. Through laughter and tears, we all learned something about each other—about what's important to each of us. This became a new tradition for the Jordan Christmas.

When our kids were younger, I started a tradition of reading the classics to them, a chapter each night. We read books like Tom Sawyer, Little Women, Rebecca of Sunnybrook Farm and Robinson Crusoe. I wish the Harry Potter books had been around for us to read together.

One tradition I heard of that I wish we had done was to plant a tree in your yard, and then, each birthday take a picture of your child in front of the tree to follow their growth. I know a grandfather who started marking a kitchen doorframe with his kids' heights forty years ago and continues to add his grandkids' measurements on there to this day. I don't know how he got his wife to okay it, but luckily, he did.

Most parents of young children worry about the teen years—"Will I be able to stay close and connected to my child when they are sixteen like I am now at six years of age?" One way to ensure that you stay connected is to create some fun one-on-one rituals with each of your kids.

I told you earlier about my ritual of taking my kids one-on-one to breakfast starting when they were in kindergarten. We went to the same restaurant, same booth and usually the same waitress. We'd play hangman or tic-tac-toe till the food came. I tried to take each of them before school about once a month. That tradition continued throughout their next 12 years until they went off to college So, it was easy to have special time with them like that during the teen years because we'd been doing it for years. It might have been harder to get a sixteen-year-old out of bed early on a school morning to go have breakfast with their old man if it wasn't such a built-in ritual.

So, start early creating these types of "dates" with each of your kids. I've always loved going with my daughter Kelly to bookstores. I fondly remember my son TJ getting me up early on a cold morning on the day after Christmas one year to ice skate on a frozen pond. I can still recall how exhilarating it was to skate on that clear, frozen pond. It became something we did every time it was cold enough for the ponds to freeze. We took some great pictures, including videos of him skating, creating another keepsake and memory.

I could go on and on but, hopefully, you get the message. We all want our kids to feel loved, special, connected and grounded. Keeping true to some old family traditions and creating some new ones of your own does just that. It is grounding to know where you come from and to be connected to your family's history. It is grounding to hear family stories over and over again and to share your own stories as well.

Keep old memories and traditions alive and make many more of your own.

Chapter 9

Family Meetings

I cannot think of a more fun and effective process to incorporate into family life than family meetings. My wife and I have been teaching parents about running family meetings in parenting classes since 1988 and have yet to find a family where parents and kids did not find them invaluable. When your family is flying by the seat of its pants, it needs a process like family meetings to bring everyone together in a tradition that creates closeness as well as creating agreements to ensure more cooperation.

First, let me give you the guidelines for how to run family meetings and then I'll fill in the gaps about their value.

Family Meeting Guidelines

1. Hold the meeting once per week at a time when everyone in the family can attend. Keep this time sacred; don't keep changing it for everyone's convenience.

2. Put all of your phones and devices in another room so there are no interruptions. This helps your children to see how valuable these meetings are to you.

3. Decisions should be made by family consensus, not by majority vote. If an agreement cannot be reached after a discussion, table the decision until the next meeting.

4. Rotate the leader for each meeting. My wife and I ran the first several meetings to model how they could run. After that, our three kids got to be the leader at every third meeting, which they loved. The leader runs the meeting and calls on members. Other members should be encouraged to support the

leader. I used to take notes on fun things that were said and what topics we discussed. A few years ago, I found my old meeting journal and shared it when our kids were all home for the holidays. This elicited lots of memories and laughs.

5. Begin the meeting with acknowledgments to each family member. Use words like, "What I love about you is..." or "I'm grateful for you because..." Teach children to say thank you after they receive a compliment. Each family member has a turn where they acknowledge everyone in the family, one at a time. At our meetings, each person ended their turn by stating one thing they loved about themselves.

6. Go on to problem-solving. "Does anyone have a problem they would like to bring up?" Teach kids that a person who is not a part of the solution is part of the problem. There should be lots of discussion and lots of give and take in coming up with solutions that work for everyone. Parents should do less talking and more listening so kids take more ownership of the meetings. If everyone agrees on a solution except for one dissenter, don't ignore their ideas—work with them. "What do you need to be okay with the agreement?" "What's not working for you?" That's how you'll gain true consensus and the respect of everyone. Kids will see over time that their voice counts and therefore, they count. And the ideas and needs of the youngest were just as important as their older sibs.

7. Consider keeping an "agenda" list on the refrigerator of issues to discuss at the next family meeting. As problems come up during the week, write them down so you remember to address them at the meeting.

8. Include a review of the next week's calendar and plan some activities together as a family. Discuss upcoming vacations or

transitions in the schedule like summer vacation and starting the school year, etc.

9. To make the meetings more productive, sit at a cleared table vs. the family room. Don't have this meeting during mealtime. You want to remove any possible distractions, especially with younger kids.

10. Always end the meeting by allowing the leader to pick a fun way to close it. This could look like choosing a bedtime snack for everyone or playing a game together.

11. If your children do not attend the meetings, check to see what you may be doing or not doing to make them not want to attend. Be honest when you check in with yourself. Have I really been listening? Have I been willing to bend and use the kids' ideas, or have I been manipulating things and not really giving kids say-so? Kids can sense when parents are open to their ideas and new ways of looking at issues vs. just going through the motions and pretending to be democratic.

12. Make an agreement with each other that if someone does not attend the meeting, that person still needs to abide by the agreements that were made at the meeting.

Acknowledging each other at the start of the meeting sets the tone. Kids, teens and parents all love to be affirmed by their loved ones. Kids get to practice giving acknowledgments and receiving them. Think how tough it is for many adults to receive praise or encouragement. Regular family meetings will allow your kids to easily take in nurturing and support from their family and friends.

We would also suggest that your first two meetings just include the acknowledgments, the activity planning, and the fun game together. Children then understand that these meetings are not just gripe sessions or for crisis management. They are fun, encouraging and empowering.

It may take some time, patience and practice for your family to learn how to create win-win agreements and to gain consensus. But, what a gift for your children to be able to acquire these skills! Just think how empowering it can be for the youngest child to be able to voice a concern and be heard and validated, and then be able to have just as much input on the final agreement as their parents and older siblings.

Parents should set the tone by getting everyone to agree that there will be no "put-downs" or criticisms during the meetings. We used to call it "no poopoo." This allows everyone to feel safe and let it all hang out. You might use your first several meetings to come up with ground rules for the meetings together. When kids can share how criticism affects them, it is more powerful than parents setting it down as a "rule."

Keep the meetings short and sweet. With young children, i.e., five- to seven-year-olds, the meetings might only last 15 minutes. With teenagers, you might go 45 minutes or longer if you are into a great discussion that matters to them. Don't let the meetings get bogged down on one issue; it is better to table it till next week vs. getting into a power struggle.

Kids are old enough and wise enough to start coming to the meetings around three to four years of age. Our son John started coming when he was just three and a half. He would beam brightly when we gave him his acknowledgments. Then, he'd get bored and wander off to play. By the time most kids are five-six, they have enough language to participate in the discussions and stay focused to handle 15 – 20 minutes, especially if the meetings are fun and they are included.

The more input that children have with the solutions or agreements about chores, bedtime, screen time, etc. the more buy-in they experience. More buy-in results in more cooperation because they have a sense of agency. The family then holds each other accountable to the agreements. It is no longer the king and queen handing down edicts. It is a democracy with shared responsibility and power. If people start slacking off on the agreements, you can bring it up at the next meeting and work out the kinks. Because the agreements are clear and the kids gave it a thumbs up, when it comes time to hold them accountable you don't need to rehash it or remind or argue; you just follow through as you told them you would. You thus avoid the constant nagging and reminding that your kids and you hate. Isn't it a lot more reasonable and tolerable to discuss chores every few months versus dealing with daily power struggles? You bet it is!

When your family is flying by the seat of its pants, it is easy for family members to feel disconnected from each other; to feel like their opinions do not count and that they are not heard. A lot of the mischief between siblings and around routines like homework, bedtime and chores is due to children feeling discouraged, disconnected from parents, and not valuable or powerful. Weekly family meetings will handle all of these areas. It only requires 20 – 40 minutes each week which even the busiest of families can find time for.

If you are a single parent, then it is just perfect for a meeting to involve just you and one child. Teenagers may grouse at first at how "weird" it sounds, but I've never had a family yet that did not report back after a handful of meetings that their teens loved the meetings and become the first ones to remind the parents about the next one.

The same goes for blended families. What better way to gain cooperation with kids who live in two different homes with two different sets of parents and siblings? Both households can hold meetings so that everyone is clear about the agreements and expectations at each home (which may differ between the two places). It allows kids a safe place to voice concerns about stepparents and for stepparents to clarify their role in issues such as discipline with their stepchildren. Being upfront and clear about agreements is an absolute necessity when dealing with blended families. Family meetings can meet these needs effectively.

With these meetings, the process is the point, not the result. What's most important is how you get to agreements, not the actual solution. What you want your children to understand is that you don't have to discuss every single issue but that all issues are discussable. Everyone is taught and encouraged to speak with authority and to get their needs met. It is equally important to be invested in everyone being heard and understood and have their needs validated and met as well. Kids learn that to create satisfying, win-win agreements, you have to both put your ideas out there and also get in the other person's shoes and see the conflict from their point of view. Everyone learns valuable skills in listening, creating consensus, working through conflicts, being held accountable, and leading a meeting.

Kids love family meetings for many reasons. One important reason is that they can have more choices and decision-making in their lives, leading to a higher sense of self-determination and autonomy. Most importantly, they feel a sense of belonging in their family. They feel heard, understood, empowered, close, and loved. If you take nothing else from this book, run weekly family meetings and reap these benefits.

Chapter 10

Boundaries and Discipline

Having an effective discipline model in place is another integral part of creating a supportive home. A family that experiences a lot of power struggles, yelling, criticism, and conflicts is not the safe base all children need. It also doesn't provide an environment where kids feel grounded and secure.

Homes where discipline and follow-through on agreements are inconsistent or absent feel chaotic, tense and out-of-control. Kids of all ages throw tantrums and rage when they don't get their way. If parents react with anger, it results in them being sucked into circular, never-ending power struggles. Parents who give in a lot feel resentful and taken advantage of; parents who yell a lot and lose it with their kids feel guilty and helpless.

The purpose of this book is not to be an all-inclusive how-to-discipline guide. But I hope this chapter serves to give you some practical ideas about how to create good cooperation at home and how to set up a long-term model for discipline.

DISCIPLINE MANTRA
Agreements with Immediate, Kind, but Firm Follow-Through Without Games or Payoffs!

A mantra is a word or short phrase that you repeat over and over again in order to create a certain state of mind. For example, in the children's book *The Little Engine That Could*, the train engine had a mantra, "I think I can," that created more courage and perseverance within her, which enabled her to climb over that steep hill.

If you incorporate my discipline mantra over and over again with your family, you will create cooperation, teamwork, empow-

erment and accountability. And, you will be making lots of deposits into your family's Goodwill Account at the same time.
Let's break down the discipline mantra into smaller pieces and discuss each one.

Agreements

As soon as kids are old enough to talk and have conversations with you, you can start involving them more and more in the agreement-making process. The more input kids have into the house agreements, the better the cooperation that will follow. That's true for kids of all ages and adults as well.

Refer back to chapter 9 on how to run regular family meetings. This is the ideal place to talk through agreements. Their ideas become incorporated into the final agreements from this healthy and respectful give-and-take process.

Everyone, parents and kids included, will walk away from a family meeting feeling good about the new agreement. Everyone will also be clear about what is expected of them and how parents will follow through. This kind of clarity is very helpful for parents because, when it does come time to follow through, there is no need for reminding and rehashing things; you took the time upfront to do that in the meeting.

Immediate, kind but firm follow-through

Following through on agreements is a challenge for many parents today. Parents don't want to yell and spank as their parents did but don't have the skills to follow through in healthier, effective ways.

But you've got to hold your kids accountable to your agreements in order to teach them that you mean what you say and to respect boundaries. Good, consistent external boundaries eventually become internal boundaries— i.e., a teen or adult's ability to discipline themselves and hold themselves accountable to their own conscience.

The **"Immediate"** word is important. It means no second, third or tenth chances. You've taken the time up front to get everyone's input and buy-in on the agreement. So, when the time comes to follow through, take action. Follow through like you said you were going to. Nagging, reminding and then finally yelling at them teaches kids the first several reminders are meaningless, and it's okay to be "parent-deaf." *I heard of a mom who one evening called to her five-year-old daughter to come down for dinner, and with each successive reminder, her voice got louder and more angry. Finally, the little girl walked into the kitchen and proclaimed, "Sorry, Mommy, I didn't hear you the first four times."*

A kind but firm approach, in my experience, works best. Being kind means being respectful, i.e., not yelling, spanking, shaming or overpowering kids into compliance. Firmness means following through no matter what. Kids naturally respect adults whose boundaries are clear and firm. They can sense a wishy-washy adult a mile away.

Firmness also means not giving in because you are tired and it's just easier to avoid any conflict that may arise when kids experience not getting their way. Bilbo Baggins, the main character in the book *The Hobbit* had a famous quote, "Short cuts make long delays." Giving in in the moment is usually easier, but, in the long run, you've created a monster.

You can be firm without yelling or scolding. Once your kids experience consistent follow-through for a while, it gets easier and easier because you've taught them that you mean what you say and there's no give in the system.

Without games or payoff

Not only must you follow through immediately in a kind, firm way, but you also have to eliminate all of the "games." By "games," I mean nagging, scolding, yelling, reminding, spanking, threatening, coaxing, pleading, bribing, arguing and renegotiating.

Believe it or not, these are all payoffs for kids. There is a tremendous sense of power and control that comes from stirring things up, getting parents frustrated or yelling, getting parents to argue with each other over their discipline, and getting parents to give in to you to avoid a tantrum. (I call this holding your family hostage). If kids can push your buttons and get you to react, there is a payoff of feeling a sense of control.

Even if kids don't get their way, there is still some payoff if they've gotten you yelling, arguing or renegotiating. And it's this feeling of being powerful and in control that will cause them to keep pushing boundaries.

If you remove all these payoffs and follow through immediately, kindly but firmly, kids get it. They learn you mean what you say, and great cooperation and accountability follow. You won't have to remind and yell anymore. And your kids will be respectful and empowered.

I encourage you to also take all the TVs, computers, video games and phones out of kids' bedrooms. It's too hard to supervise what they are watching and playing and for how long. Those devices are best placed in family rooms or kitchens where you can monitor them by walking by every so often. It's just good common sense.

Use your weekly family meeting to create clear, win-win agreements and then follow through consistently without all the "games." Kids feel more secure when they have well-defined, consistent boundaries and parents feel more confident and calm as well.

For more information on redirecting and preventing power struggles, see my previous book: *Food Fights & Bedtime Battles: A Working Parents Guide to Negotiating Daily Power Struggles.*

Chapter 11

Opportunities to Grow

The teacher noticed little Tommy was withdrawn and anxious. "What are you so worried about?" Tommy: "It's my parents. My dad works all day to keep me clothed and fed and sent to the best school, and he's working overtime to be able to send me to college. My Mom spends all day cooking and cleaning and shopping so that I have nothing to worry about." Teacher: "Then why are you worried?" Tommy: "I'm afraid they may try to escape!"

For me, kids being "grounded" also means feeling capable, confident and knowing that you can take care of yourself. It is a knowingness that comes from experience— experiences where you have overcome obstacles and persevered.

My concern is that today's parents are so fearful and protective that they are not allowing kids these growth and character-building experiences. Parents are so worried about kidnappings and that their children are going to fall behind their peers that they overprotect and micromanage kids.

There is an old expression that "What you protect you make weak." I'm concerned we are keeping our kids young and weak too often.

Free play began to decline in the 1980s and accelerated in the 1990s. Parents began to fear kidnappers and sex offenders; the term "stranger danger" didn't appear in English-language books until the early 1980s.

"Good judgment comes from experience and often experience comes from bad judgment." (Rita Mae Brown)

I love that quote because it is so true. Kids growing up in the 50's, 60's, and 70's had a lot more freedom and unsupervised time than today's kids. If you don't believe me, think back to your own experiences growing up and remember what you and your friends were allowed to do that you don't allow your kids to experience today.

I can remember riding my bike at age ten with my two older brothers and neighborhood kids five miles down a busy four-lane road, parking our bikes at a shopping center, getting on the Redbird Express city bus and riding about twenty-five miles downtown to the Cardinals baseball games. We'd then take the bus back to the shopping center, hop on our bikes and race home at dusk.

There is no way any parent today would let their kids do that! Too many worries about kidnappings or getting hit by a car. We've developed a belief that our kids must always be safe, not make mistakes or fail, and shouldn't be in situations where they might get hurt. Oh, and they must always be reachable and answer our texts and check in every hour. But just think about all of the invaluable lessons kids are missing out on because they lack these experiences. Some fascinating research demonstrated that the risk of injury per hour of unsupervised physical play is lower than the risk per hour of playing adult-guided sports while conferring many more developmental benefits.

Play with some degree of physical risk is essential because it teaches children how to look after themselves and each other. Kids will take on responsibility for their safety when they are actually responsible for their safety, rather than relying on the adult guardians hovering over them.

Parents have long feared any new trend or experiences with teens: dime novels, cars, comic books, rock and roll records, drive-in movies, TV, video games, the mall, computers, the internet, cell phones, and social networking sites.

The following are some of the things parents have feared since the 1980s: stranger danger, online predators, abductions, youth gangs in the 1980s, teen predators and juvenile delinquents, drugs, heroin, AIDs, STDs, premarital sex, teen pregnancy, early puberty, hooking up, vaping, decreasing society norms and values, other parents who don't monitor or control their kids, working parents with latchkey kids, the war on drugs, online predators and sexual predators, and pornography. The media and 24/7 news cycle have blown many of these fears out of proportion to reality, including our fears that our kids will be abducted. This fear flies in the face of data that shows that compared to the 1970s and 1980s, there are much fewer kidnappings today than at that time. The following are some of the **benefits to kids** when they are allowed opportunities to grow.

1. Kids learn to make choices/decisions for themselves and then to immediately experience the consequences of their choices. Learning these natural consequences out in the real world is so much more meaningful than our warnings and lectures.

"One thorn of experience is worth a whole wilderness of warning." (James Lowell-writer)

2. Kids learn how to lead and to follow the leader. When kids are out and about without adults constantly looking over their shoulders, it forces them into leadership roles. They must think for themselves, make decisions, and chart their own course.

3. Kids learn how to take care of themselves. They learn to be responsible for themselves and their actions. They learn to take care of siblings and friends. Kids also develop the confidence and ability to solve their own problems.

4. Kids learn how to entertain themselves. Instead of whining about being bored, they can channel their energies into making

things happen, taking initiative, creating their own teams and rules for their games, and creating their own fun. Some of my fondest memories from growing up come from all the games we played out in the street and in the woods and skating on frozen creeks and ponds.

When our son John was in fifth grade, he asked if he could ride his bike up to a pizza parlor with his friends. My wife and I's first reaction was terror! I mean, think of all the things that could go wrong! I'm exaggerating a little.

But instead, we gracefully recovered and remembered all of the valuable things that could go right in letting him ride his bike one mile down a residential street. We did ride behind him the first time so he could show us he knew how to stop at side streets, find the place etc. And then we let him go. And the results were predictable. He and his buddies had a blast! They'd ride there in a little posse, park their bikes, buy their pizzas and drinks and feel like grownups. They were beside themselves one day when, after many visits to this pizza place, the manager gave them free breadsticks! For ten-year-old boys, that is nirvana! Free food! Wow! The manager knows us! Big stuff!

Most importantly, they were proud of themselves. They were out on their own, having fun and taking care of themselves and each other.

5. Collaboration: The way my friends and I decided which team got to bat first in our neighborhood baseball games was not to call our mom or dad to come out and decide. We'd toss a bat to our opponent, he'd catch it with one hand, then we'd alternate grabbing the bat just above the last person's hand until someone would place his hand over the knob and that decided the winner. Unsupervised play forces kids to solve conflicts, make up the rules of the game they are playing,

police themselves, and develop other invaluable social skills like handling teasing.

6. Risks: Children need the opportunity to face and assess risks. That's the best way for them to develop the ability to judge risk and to take appropriate action that situations require. Kids need to stretch themselves, test themselves, and challenge themselves in order to know who they are and what they can accomplish. And, they discover that when things go wrong, even if they get hurt, they can usually handle it without calling in an adult. Here's an insightful story that makes this point.

Two girls were playing far away from their village when one of them, 10 years old, fell into a well. Her friend was a 6-year-old, skinny kid. She tied a rope onto a bucket and lowered it into the well. She then pulled and pulled with all her might, her hands becoming blistered and bloody, but she never quit until her friend was pulled out. When they returned to the village, no one believed their story. "How could a skinny, 6-year-old save a large 10-year-old?" The girls insisted it was true, so they asked the old, local wise man. He believed them and said the truth was very simple. There was no adult there to tell her she couldn't do it.
Develop resilience:

'*The purpose of obstacles is to INSTRUCT, not OBSTRUCT*"
(Mark Rosenberg- speaker)

One of the best learning processes for kids is to try something, fail, get frustrated, try again, fail, get frustrated, try again and succeed! And then to be able to say to themselves, "I DID IT!"

It is healthy and necessary for kids to sometimes get frustrated, suffer, and to be unhappy. Those feelings and experiences are when we gain our motivation and when we experience the value of persevering. It's when we build character.

What you protect, you make weak. Stop overprotecting your kids and doing too much for them. The writer John Ruskin once said, *"The highest reward for a person's toil is not what they get for it, but what they become by it."* That's so true, isn't it? Allow your kids some growing pains and watch them flourish.

"A man begins cutting his wisdom teeth the first time he bites off more than he can chew." (Herb Coen, journalist). We've got to let kids make mistakes and learn from them, take some risks and learn from them, and suffer sometimes and grow from it. And on the flip side, make good choices, take care of yourself, succeed and experience the intrinsic pride and fulfillment from a job well done.

So take a good hard look at yourselves as parents. Make note of anything you are doing for your kids that they can/should be doing for themselves and turn it over to them. If you're not sure of their ability to handle something, take a little time to teach/train them and then turn it over, let go and watch them flourish.

Also, be sure you are allowing your kids to have enough freedom and opportunities to build character and take care of themselves. If you're not willing to let your kids do some of the things your parents allowed you to do, then what will you replace it with? I cringe when I see that most middle schoolers' free space is walking around the mall with their friends. I guess that is their version of our "woods" and "neighborhood fun."

Look for opportunities to let go a little and let kids prove to you and themselves that they can handle freedoms and time away from you. Find safe places where they can stretch, explore, initiate and create for themselves.

In order for kids to be "grounded" today as in past generations, they need to build upon experiences that reinforce within them that they are capable, that they can make good choices, and that they can take care of themselves. Kids who have learned street smarts, overcome obstacles, met challenges and found their strength and motivation from within can overcome any future obstacles or frustrations. That is the only way for them to develop grit, resilience, and an optimistic attitude. They will have learned that they can overcome obstacles because they have been allowed to do it throughout their childhood.

A healthy human childhood with a lot of autonomy and unsupervised play in the real world sets children's brains to operate mostly in what author Jonathon Haidt calls "discover mode," with a well-developed attachment system and an ability to handle the risks of daily life.

One final quote to leave you with. *"Experience is a hard teacher...she gives the test first* and *the lessons afterward."*

Chapter 12

Chores, Homework, Allowance and Other Everyday Matters

Okay, we talked about family meetings in chapter 9, and we've talked about a discipline model. So, how do I specifically get my kid to do their chores? Or their homework? Should I pay my kids to do chores? How should I set up an allowance with them? I'll answer these questions and more in this chapter using the framework provided by previous chapters.

If you've been making regular deposits into the Goodwill Account with your kids, accountability and cooperation happen much more easily. If you've had effective weekly family meetings, your kids should feel empowered, have a sense of agency, and thus be open to making good agreements about chores and homework. And if you've been good at doing your discipline mantra and following through consistently with your discipline, you will have removed most of the boundary-pushing and resistance.

So, let's tackle a few specific issues that can cause families grief and recurrent struggles.

Chores

Having to "do it all" is one of the main problems that cause parents not to feel grounded. About 70% of moms are in the workforce today, so, for most families, the days of having mom home to cook, clean and pick up after everyone are long gone. Allowing kids to not pitch in to help with meals, cleaning and helping with their siblings should not be an option. As I've said previously, exhausted, crabby, impatient and resentful parents make poor disciplinarians. I'd suggest that mom and dad make up a list (with or without their kid's help) of all the things that need to be done around the house every day and every week. Decide which things you'd like the kids to help with. Then, sit down at a family meeting and tell the kids that you need help, why you need help, what help you need, and ask them how they'd like to contribute.

You might ask each child to pick 2 to 3 things from the list, perhaps negotiating with their siblings about who does what. I know several families that have a "chore jar" filled with little pieces of paper with one chore written on each piece. Every week or once a month, each family member picks three pieces of paper blindly, and those become their chores until the next drawing.

Before we got our dog, Mamie, years ago, we had our then 6-year-old son and 7-year-old daughter brainstorm all the jobs that having a dog would entail, i.e., feeding, taking her out to go to do her business three times a day, exercise, cleaning, etc. They negotiated who would do what, and after Mamie arrived, they enthusiastically went to work at their new jobs.

As you might expect, after a month or so, they slacked off. We re-discussed the dog duties at another family meeting, and they were good again for many months. Over the past 14 years, the kids have redefined who does what and when with the dog, but it's always worked out that better cooperation follows. And it has kept Anne and I out of having to remind and nag every day about the dog.

Kids can do their own laundry or help with it, vacuum, dust, clean bathrooms, clean their own rooms, empty and load dishwashers, help with meal preparation and clean up, babysit siblings and help with yard work. In family meetings, you can get clear with them about when their chores are to be done and how, and all of this is done through a give-and-take discussion as previously discussed.

And despite some normal grousing and groaning about having to do chores, especially since "None of my friends have to do chores," there are many tremendous benefits to kids from doing them. First and perhaps most importantly, they are making an important contribution to their family. It feels good to know you are helping out and being valuable. I think it's good for anyone living in your house to pitch in. They'll learn that it's part of living together in a community. This attitude will carry over when they are living in a dorm room or an apartment during college.

When kids can meet their responsibilities, they feel more confident and capable. For kids, knowing from lots of experience that you can mow the lawn, do your laundry or prepare a meal is empowering. Research has shown that most kids today who leave home to start college have never balanced a checkbook, cooked a meal or washed their own clothes. Chores prepare kids for the real world.

One day Billy was left to fix his own lunch. When his mom returned home with a friend, she noticed he had already strained the tea. "Did you find the tea strainer?" Billy: "No, so I just used the flyswatter." Mom nearly fainted, so Billy quickly added, "Don't worry, Mom, I used an old one."

They'll never learn important life skills unless they are taught and given the opportunity to practice them.

I would also encourage you not to pay kids for doing these household chores. Paying them takes away the intrinsic good feelings from helping out. Rewards can also quickly become a complicated manipulation game on both sides. When parents have trained their kids to expect rewards, their first response when asked to help with something is to put their hand out and ask you what they're going to get for it. Parents end up using the money as a threat and a manipulation, which almost always backfires. So don't start down this path.

Allowance

This brings us to the discussion of allowance. Should you or shouldn't you? I think the better question would be, "What's your intention behind giving an allowance?"

I'd suggest that the intention is to teach them about money: how to save money, the value of money and how to budget money. When you're at the store, and your child points to a Lego set and says, "I want you to buy me that," you can calmly tell them, "I'm not willing to buy that for you. But if you really want it, you can save up your money and get it for yourself. Let's see how much it costs. Oh, gosh, it's sixty dollars; you'll have to start saving your money and probably earn some extra, too!"

Kids learn firsthand what things cost and the value of them. And they will learn to delay gratification, which I'm afraid happens all too seldom today.

I heard a story about three boys who were bragging about their fathers after a church service one Sunday. The first boy bragged, "My dad scribbles a few words on paper, calls it a poem, and gets $1000 for it." The second boy, trying to one-up his buddy, said, "That's nothing, my dad scribbles a few words on a paper, calls it a song, and gets $2000." The last boy grinned and said, "I've got you both beat. My dad scribbles a few words on paper, calls it a sermon, and it takes four people to collect all the money." Yes, our kids for sure need to learn about money.

When our kids were in grade school, we gave them an allowance of about ten to fifteen dollars per month. Once they were in middle school, they asked for more at a family meeting. After much debate, we decided to give them thirty-five dollars a month, but they were now responsible for buying lunch at school if they wanted to buy lunch and paying for movie tickets and other weekend fun when out with their friends. They could always pack lunch from home on us, and if we went to the movies as a family, we paid. But all the extras and their fun money was on them.

The first month on the new allowance plan, Kelly blew her thirty-five bucks after just one week and she came to us for some lunch money. The answer, of course, was no. And we hoped she'd learned something about budgeting her money for the next month (which she did!).

We also opened up a savings account for each of them and encouraged them to put a portion of any money they received into their savings account. We talked with them about how they'd be responsible for future car insurance and buying their own car. Plus they'd have to help pay for part of their college fees.

I strongly suggest that allowance NOT be tied to doing chores, as I explained earlier in this chapter. Don't use it to coerce, threaten or manipulate. I'd give them enough to learn the lessons about money but not so much that they aren't a little hungry. *You want kids to develop ambition, like the boy who sat on the side of the road with his fishing line down a drain. Feeling sorry for him, a lady gave him $5 and asked, "How many have you caught?" The boy grinned and said, "You're the 10th so far this AM."* Compare that ambition with this teenager.

The teacher asked the class to write an essay on what they would do if they were given a million dollars. Johnny handed in a blank sheet of paper. The teacher said, "Johnny, you haven't done anything. How come?" His response was, "Because that's exactly what I'd do if I had a million dollars." That's the result of overindulging kids.

I've found over the years that kids love learning about money and having their own. It's very empowering for them and makes them feel more grown up and responsible.

Investment

Teacher: "If you had $10 and you asked your dad for $10 more, how many dollars would you have?"
Johnny: "$10."
Teacher: "You don't know your addition tables."
Johnny: "You don't know my dad."

It's also a good idea to find ways for your kids to be invested in their activities. For example, when our son T.J.'s hockey fees went up to about a thousand dollars for the season, we told him we wanted him to contribute to paying for part of it. Soccer cost sixty-five dollars comparatively. So he started out at about eleven years of age, paying a hundred dollars per season, eventually paying two hundred per season by eighth grade. In high school, the students who sold enough ads for the hockey programs had to pay zero for hockey, and every season, he hustled and sold ads and, therefore, avoided having to pay any fees. I guarantee you he not only never missed a practice, even at the five a.m. time slots, but he was the first player on the ice because he loved hockey and because he had some investment in it.

T.J. started pestering us around age seven for us to buy him a video game set. I hated the idea of it, so I said, "No, we don't want to have one in our house." At age ten, my wife and T.J. ambushed me once again, asking for us to buy a set. We finally compromised, with Anne and I saying he could have one, but only if he bought the whole thing himself.

Well, about six months later that little stinker had scrimped and saved and worked and earned the one hundred and fifty dollars it cost back then for his Nintendo set. And like with his hockey investment, he was really proud to tell people about how he had bought his Nintendo all by himself. It really was empowering for him.

So, stop giving, giving, giving! Find ways for your kids to be earning, earning, earning! I told our son John (I must sound like Scrooge) we weren't willing to pay for him to play paintball. But we told him he could go if he paid for it himself. He only went two or three times at his friend's special birthday parties, even though for a while there, his friend's parents were buying them guns and for them to go several times a month. When John went, it was a lot more meaningful because he was paying for it. He also was very creative in borrowing equipment and finding deals on the paintballs. Sweat equity and having some skin in the game are wonderful learning experiences.

Homework

Son: "Here's my report card, Dad, along with one of your old ones I found in the attic.

Dad: "Well, son, you're right, this old report card of mine isn't any better than yours. I guess the only fair thing is to give you what my dad gave me.

Just a few words on schoolwork. Decide early on, in first grade, who is responsible for their school work. That person should be the student, not you! Stay out of the habit of being too involved in the everyday work, nagging about assignments or doing work for them.

Read with your kids, quiz them on spelling words and be available to answer questions, but don't do it for them. Don't be more motivated and responsible than they are. *Kids who have parents who remind them a lot don't have to remember.* If you teach your kids by your actions that you will rescue and pick up the pieces for them, they will never learn to be self-responsible and self-motivated. This has become much harder for parents to live out because schools have online sites like Infinite Campus, where they post students' progress every day on homework assignments and test grades. It can be excruciatingly hard not to step in when you see an assignment that is missing or late or see that they received a low mark on a test. What you want to avoid is knowing more and caring more about the child's schoolwork than they do. I encourage parents to sit down with each child every week or so and go over their progress. Ask what subjects they enjoy and why. Have them show you their work and their grades. If their scores have dropped in a subject, ask them how they feel about that and what their plan is for addressing it. I teach girls in my counseling practice to "focus on the journey vs. the destination." The destination is their grades; the journey is the study strategies and the normal amount of time they have learned they need to put into their studying to get the results they want. Let them do the problem-solving and do not rescue them or use it as an excuse to restart micromanaging.

If your 6th grader is missing some assignments and the teacher calls, I'd suggest you hand the phone to your twelve-year-old and let them deal with the consequences of their actions. If your 9th grader is having trouble with a teacher, encourage them to set up a meeting with the teacher. Let them work it out by expressing their feelings and their needs and coming to some agreement about making changes.

The earlier you start turning over responsibility to your kids for schoolwork, the easier it will be because you avoid years of having been the main motivator and the one taking charge. I have seen far too many 18-year-olds go off to college and not have a clue about how to fend for themselves academically. At that point, the consequences are much larger and more expensive.

Another important aspect of this process is that when your child brings home a good report card, **they** own it, not you. They feel the self-satisfaction and pride that comes from overcoming obstacles and working hard. What a great way to support your child's intrinsic motivation.

There are lots of ways to show you care about their education and schooling. Be involved with their class and their school. Help out in the classroom and go on field trips. Get to know the teachers and support staff. Let your kids see that you continue educating yourself with books, classes and retreats. Talk indirectly over the years about the value of education using real-life examples from relatives, friends and people in the news. And yet again, your example is so important.

I hope you see the character-building value of kids being allowed to be helpful and valuable at home. And how proud and competent they will feel when they learn to be responsible for their homework, laundry, hygiene and boredom. And how invaluable it is for kids to have some personal investment in their activities. Use your family meetings to work through agreements about issues like chores, homework and allowance, and watch your kids grow up from all of these experiences. And cultivate a habit to stop doing for kids anything that they are ready and able to do for themselves.

Chapter 13

Youth Sports

In my experience, one of the biggest disruptors of family balance today is youth sports. The way youth sports have changed over the past 100 years, especially the past 20 years, has undermined character development and family equilibrium. Sports have gotten more cutthroat and competitive among kids and parents, with a resultant dramatic rise in overuse injuries, burnout, anxiety, and the pressure to hyperspecialize earlier and younger. Participating in youth sports today has become very expensive and time consuming, leaving behind many middle- and lower-class kids. Parents in the wealthiest households spent about four times more on their child's sport than the lowest-income families (*State of Play 2022* report). In 2024, surveyed children from low-income households were three times less likely to play on traveling teams than those from high-income homes. And it can end up taking over a family's life.

I've been involved with sports ever since I was in grade school. I played ice hockey and football throughout high school and also played tennis for my college team. When my kids were growing up, I helped coach soccer, basketball and ice hockey. So, I love sports and what it can bring to kids. What I'm not a fan of is the involvement of kids in club sports, and here's why.

Organized youth sports began in the early 1900s as a way to teach "American" values like respect, cooperation, hard work and respect for authority, preparing kids for the new industrial society that needed physical laborers to work in factories. Due to the high levels of new immigrants in cities, urban reformers became concerned with poor immigrant boys who, because of overcrowding in tenements, were often on the streets. Reformers saw sports leagues as a means to keep underprivileged boys off the streets and out of trouble, and newly established parks and playgrounds provided viable space. Interestingly, in the 1920s and 1930s many physical education professionals called the organizational focus on competition harmful, putting too much emphasis on athletic talent at too young an age. As a result, most organized competition left the public elementary school system.

Fast forward to the 1960s when the self-esteem movement began to take hold in schools, with its focus on building confidence and talent without too much competition or comparison between children. Its reach didn't extend to outside activities, and parents increasingly wanted more competitive opportunities for their children and were willing to pay for them.

The 1960s also gave rise to growing competition over college admissions. Campuses were bursting with Baby Boom-generation students. Top schools couldn't meet the demand, which meant that everyone would not be accepted into college. Increasingly anxious parents began to focus on athletics as a means by which their kids could gain admission to quality universities. The 1970s, 80s and 90s saw families become more competitive and afterschool activities for kids continued to develop, evolve and intensify, particularly in the 1990s. Another key factor in this issue was the rapid rise in the cost of a college education. The skyrocketing cost of higher education became one of the main drivers of the professionalization of youth sports to achieve the dream of free college.

I believe the other major driver of what I consider to be out-of-control youth sports is that parents and money have become overly involved. The U.S. youth sports economy—which includes everything from travel to private coaching to apps that organize leagues and livestream games—was worth $37.5 billion by 2022 and is estimated to reach $69.4 billion by 2030. Municipalities that used to vie for minor-league teams are now banking on youth sports to boost local economies. Towns began issuing bonds for lavish sports complexes that they hope will lure young athletes and their families. Youth sports are being privatized, and a lot of people are making a lot of money from it.

One consequence of this race to make money off of kids is that our children are suffering because of it. There has been a growing body of research showing that intense early specialization in a single sport increases the risk of injury, burnout and depression. In a 2016 study published in the journal *Family Relations*, Dorsch and his colleagues found that the more money families pour into youth sports, the more pressure their kids feel and the less they enjoy and feel committed to their sport. The more parents pay, the more emotionally invested they become in the outcome of the games. Youth sports officials tell me how much more intense and abusive parents have become, and there has been a resultant lack of officials willing to officiate games.

Another harm experienced by kids is overuse injuries, whose numbers have skyrocketed in the past 30 years. Young athletes who participated in their primary sport for more than eight months in a year were more likely to report overuse injuries. An estimated 50% of all sports-related injuries in kids result from overuse. Despite warnings from the American Academy of Pediatrics and the American Academy of Orthopedic Surgeons, coaches are still pushing kids to focus on one sport. At a critical phase of developmental growth, when children should be naturally developing balance, coordination, agility and spatial awareness, they are being forced instead to overtrain and perform specialized movements that create muscular imbalances and deficiencies within their body that result in overuse injuries.

Kids as young as 8-10 years of age are being pushed to specialize in one sport, which then develops into playing that sport year-round. The American Academy of Pediatrics found that burnout, anxiety, depression and attrition are increased in early specializers. Studies have shown that delaying specialization in most cases until late adolescence increases the likelihood of athletic success. In a survey of 296 NCAA Division I male and female athletes, UCLA researchers discovered that 88% played an average of two to three sports as children.

During a church service one Sunday morning, a minister asked the congregation who wanted to go to heaven after today's service. Everyone in the church raised their hand except for a young boy in the front row. The minister kindly looked down at him and asked, "Son, don't you want to go to heaven?" The little boy responded, "Yes, sir, I'd like to, but I have soccer practice at two."

The business of youth sports has made a year-long training schedule hyperspecializing in one sport the new norm. And new select traveling club teams have further extended a child's time playing the game, conditioning coaches and parents to believe that more is better when it comes to practice, games and tournaments. Kids as young as middle school now perform at elite showcases in front of higher-level club and college coaches, and that reinforces the need to train during the off-season and year-round.

About 70% of young athletes give up on youth sports by age 13. And the primary reason is that it was not fun anymore. Kids point to coaches who were too intense and overly focused on winning, overzealous parents and the lack of free time to hang out with friends. Young athletes may experience emotional problems by practicing too much, playing the same sport all the time or pushing themselves to be perfect. High-stakes sports take something that was supposed to be a stress outlet and reducer and turns it into something that is a source of stress and anxiety.

I have counseled so many athletes, most commonly in early to mid-high school, who are miserable playing their sport. But they don't quit because they are so afraid of disappointing their parents, coaches and teammates. They worry that their parents would be disappointed because they have invested so much money and time and sacrificed weekends and vacations for their sport. It feels like there is no off-ramp for them.

There are many girls in grade school through high school who are sorely disappointed when they can't come to one week of my summer camp because their coach won't let them miss one practice or game. Parents lament that their child's coach has the power to dictate their summer schedule and vacations. Some kids play as many as 50-70 baseball or softball games in a summer. That includes out-of-town tournaments most weekends. I hate that families have given so much power to these coaches and youth sports!

So, how can your child enjoy sports and gain the lessons from participating in them and also stay in balance? Is it possible to keep your family grounded in the face of these pressures? I say yes, and here's how.

First and foremost, refuse to get caught up in the current rat race of college scholarship or bust, being the best, hyper-specializing in the same sport year-round, focusing on winning and being on the best club teams. I described earlier how your family can create its own end in mind, i.e., your family values. Use these values to guide decisions about their involvement in sports. Our family's agreement was one sport a season and not hyperspecializing until at least 10th or 11th grade. Our goal wasn't to produce professional athletes or violin players. We believed childhood was about way more important things like developing social-emotional skills, becoming well-rounded, sampling lots of different activities so that they could learn what they loved, working a job, and God forbid, enjoying some unsupervised, fun, free time with friends.

It's important to note that what might be more important than what our children are doing with these sports is what they are not doing. What we are losing is the era of sandlot or pickup ball, a form of play that organically promoted innovation and fitness among generations of Americans. More than 40% of parents whose child plays an organized sport say their child does so year-round (RWJF/Harvard/NPR, 2015). Yet free play has been shown to produce higher levels of physical activity than organized sports, plus all of the benefits we discussed in chapter 11.

Here are some reality check statistics regarding the rat race to playing college sports. Only 2% of high school athletes go on to play at the top level of college sports, the NCAA's Division I. Only about 5-6% of high school athletes compete at any National Collegiate Athletic Association (NCAA) level, and fewer than 2% receive an athletic scholarship. Most student-athletes are not on "full rides" that cover all education costs. Only about 1% of them are on full scholarships. These numbers include Division 1, 2 and 3. The bottom line is that you actually have a better chance of getting more money by earning good grades and test scores than by being a good athlete. To put the icing on this cake, one final stat: only 0.3% to 0.4% of high school athletes make it to the professional level.

Stick to only allowing kids to play one sport a season. Follow guidelines by the American Academy of Pediatrics and the American Academy of Orthopedic Surgeons that state that kids should not play or train more than 5 days a week. They should also have at least 3 to 4 months off from any given sport during the year. These breaks can be divided into one-month breaks when they can focus on other activities or free play and have time for cross-training, flexibility, core strength or recovery. Athletes can avoid injuries by trying different activities that work different muscle groups and parts of the body.

Coaches, especially in the beginning years, should be kind and fun with an emphasis on having fun, learning some skills and learning how to be a supportive teammate. At every age and level, choose coaches with good intentions, i.e., not solely focused on winning or producing college athletes. Do the best you can to get to know the other parents, discuss what everyone's intentions are for the season, and communicate those desires to the coaches so that *YOU* take charge of your child's experience. When I coached my son's middle school hockey team, I'd discuss out-of-town tournament possibilities with the parents before the season started. Most parents were fine with 1-2 of these per season, so we would stick to that even if other opportunities came up.

Make sure kids are pursuing a sport because of their reasons vs. wanting to please or not disappoint parents. Ask kids why they like their sport so you can hear their intrinsic reasons for wanting to play. Listen to them if they express burnout, make sure they feel heard and understood, and let them choose their activities and levels. They can play 20 games a season vs. 60 and still derive the benefits of playing.

Value the need for breaks, family vacations and non-sport camps like mine. Have recurrent conversations about the value of balance: make sure athletics are balanced with other activities like music, the arts, jobs, family time, downtime and time to follow other interests. Our kids, along with Anne and I, decided on a one-sport-a-season agreement in order to ensure downtime and our sanity. Remember the story from the "Begin with the End in Mind" chapter about how we stood our ground with our son TJ only getting to play one sport a season. That's the value of making these kinds of commitments at a time when there is no pressure and everyone is clear-headed.

Also, occasionally check in with your child about whether they still enjoy their sport. Make sure there are clear off-ramps so they avoid burnout and avoid doing things solely to please you.

Parents and kids can overdo any extracurricular activity, be it dance, competitive cheer, robotics, music or theater. I chose athletics to focus on because I see more kids out of balance with their club sports teams than any other activity. It is so healthy for kids to try activities outside of their main thing. I encourage athletes to be part of a play and marching band kids to try a sport. A variety of activities and interests makes them a more interesting person.

Chapter 14
Technology and Social Media

A couple was heading to the hospital with their 16-year-old daughter, who was scheduled to undergo a tonsillectomy. During the ride, they talked about the procedure. "Dad," the teenager asked, "how are they going to keep my mouth open during surgery?" Without hesitation, her father quipped, "They're going to give you your phone."

In this chapter, I hope to give you some new ways of deciding when kids are ready for smartphones and social media. I'll start with a historical perspective to remind you that new forms of communication for the past 2000 years have always brought an initial phase of worry about their effects on children, adults and society. I'll then take you for a stroll down memory lane to remind you of how *YOU* hung out with your friends and what kids are missing out on in today's busy, overly supervised and restrictive environment. I will then offer you some specific recommendations about how to know when your child is ready to start using devices and social media. Finally, you will learn some important factors to consider in how to actually prepare them to begin. I have placed my favorite books on this topic in the bibliography, so you can read those if you want more in-depth information. Let's get started.

The most impactful things that affected and changed parenting in the past 20 years are the rapid spread of high-speed broadband in the 2000s, the introduction of the iPhone in 2007, and the new age of social media. Parents and kids have been entertained, hooked, distracted and reeling ever since. Let me give you a brief historical perspective on the initial reaction to and the effects of previous new forms of communication that suddenly made it easier for people to connect across larger spaces and time. Each new creation generated angst about its effects on people and society.

Believe it or not, when written language arrived on the scene in Greece around 400 BC, people worried writing would make people forget more easily and that it would dumb people down. Miraculously, we actually found it allowed you to experience ideas in private, in a more reflective way. Go figure. The printing press' introduction in 1432 made people unsettled because it created so much more information and caused people to be more distracted.

The telegraph and railroads arrived in the 1840s, and the Pony Express connected people with '"instant" communication. You could even receive these communications at home. The next worrisome development was industrialization and the move to cities. Citizens felt out-of-control and busier, and they now had to contend with an environment that was noisier, more crowded, and that required work outside the home, especially for men.

Next to arrive was telegrams and then the telephone. All of these new technologies were considered better than nothing if you couldn't meet face-to-face. This was a similar sentiment that we heard about our devices and social media during the pandemic. Radio and TV created the mass media, and society worried we were losing ourselves and our ability to think for ourselves. In 1970, Alvin Toffler, the author of *Future Shock*, coined the phrase "information overload," which in the past two decades has taken on new life.

Answering machines let us decide who we wanted to respond to or ignore, becoming a screening device as it let voice mail pick up messages. Email gave us more control over who, how and when we responded to people, but then this became too slow.

Texts were faster and in real-time, but they became constant and exhausting.

Video games had their day in the sun, i.e., the cause of more angst about the effects on our children's brains, mental health and attention spans. Since the arrival of smartphones and social media, everyone—parents, the education system and mental health experts alike—has been on full alert about their deleterious effects on children and teenagers.

This is not to downplay the harmful effects of social media and phones, but it does give me pause to remember that every new communication device brings an initial wave of concern over its effects on people. Over time, people adjust their usage and learn how to use them without being harmed. I think we are in the process of that learning curve today with our devices.

Technology continues to change at an alarming pace, as this story suggests: *In a restaurant, a mother noticed her eleven-year-old daughter staring at a movie poster on the wall. The picture portrayed Superman standing in a phone booth. The girl's mother whispered to her husband, "I don't think she knows who Superman is." He told her it was worse than that. "She doesn't know what a phone booth is."*

I have a few questions for parents: Where did you get together with friends? How much free time did you have? How busy were you, and how much homework did you suffer with? What freedoms and unsupervised time did you enjoy, and what were the lessons you learned from them? Your answers to these questions will highlight the different kinds of childhood your children are experiencing today.

Where did parents get together? Most parents and grandparents of today's children were allowed more freedom and less supervision from adults, and they enjoyed more public spaces to hang out. These included the streets in their neighborhoods and beyond, the woods, malls, fast food joints, skating rinks, other neighborhoods, drive-in movies, phone calls, football games, dances and public spaces like parks. We hung out with our friends and met new ones at all of those spaces. This allowed unsupervised time with peers without adults peeking over our shoulders or hearing our conversations. It was so nice to have that kind of privacy where we could hang with who we wanted to hang with, swap secrets, flirt, etc.

How much free time did you have? Way more than today's kids. We didn't have traveling club youth sports teams, competitive dance and cheer, nor the myriad enrichment activities kids are forced to endure today. Kids, especially in the lower grades, had less homework. We didn't have ACT prep classes and weren't made to retake those tests 2-4 times. I don't ever remember any kid missing playing ball in the street because they had a Suzuki violin lesson or a Kumon math session.

What kind of freedoms did you enjoy? Coming from a family of eight kids, my mom shushed us out the door and we were told not to come home until dinner in order to not awaken younger napping siblings. We were out and about all day long. We rode our bikes miles away, crossed 4-lane highways, and played ice hockey on frozen ponds we walked to in zero-degree weather. We spent idyllic afternoons hiking through some woods near our house, shooting BB and pellet guns and setting off M-80s and cherry bomb fireworks. We never checked in with our parents because they trusted we knew how to take care of ourselves and each other. And we did. Oh, and parents didn't usually feel the need to monitor how much time teens spent talking to friends and dating partners on the landline phone.

What do kids experience today? Because of the parental fears I highlighted in chapter 11, kids today are tethered to a short leash. We have shrunken their geographic freedom along with giving them less free time and downtime. More worry and restrictions have come with increased curfew and loitering laws and limited mobility. Parents feel pressure to keep kids busy so that they don't get into trouble. This leads to more supervised activities and hectic schedules. And so the only place kids and teens can hang out is online. We've forced them to socialize online because of their shrunken geographic freedoms and their busy schedules. Social networking sites have become the only public spaces to get together with some measure of privacy and autonomy.

When a kid goes outside on a typical weekend afternoon, there is no one to play with because friends are at tournaments, many of them out of town. Many teens elect to stay home on weekend nights because they are so tired and stressed out from their frenetic weekday schedules. So, they sit on their beds scrolling through social media online.

Parents have been conditioned to believe they have to monitor everything to be a good parent. From a teen's perspective, it feels like they are being micromanaged, controlled and smothered. Teens tell me this conveys a lack of trust and a sense that their parents don't really know them. Many kids tell me they end up stuck at home because of their parent's work schedules, along with parental fears for their safety.

What do kids today want? Pretty much the same things we wanted when we were growing up. They desire informal gatherings with diverse groups of peers without adult supervision on their terms. They need places to gossip, complain, flirt, catch up, meet new people, compare notes, jockey for status, and fall in love. They won't experience this by being involved in school activities. Teens would much rather hang out in person than be online. For the most part, they are compelled by friendships and closeness, not gadgets; devices are just a means to an end.

Your children want you to believe the facts that show that the world is safe enough for most kids to be outside and down the street. They want you to let go so they can prove that they are capable of handling themselves without your constant supervision. Kids want you to remember the freedoms you got to experience. And that although your parents did not know your every move and whereabouts, you managed. They want to be allowed to learn street smarts and to manage their friendships and social lives on their own.

Opportunities to access public spaces for socializing has historically been an important part of growing up, allowing kids to take risks, explore and have adventures, and develop self-determination. You don't experience this or learn these lessons when you spend most of your free time on digital streets. Review the lessons kids learn when they are given more freedom and unsupervised time in chapter 11.

So, with that as our backdrop, how can you tell when your child is ready for a phone or to be on social media? I'll give you more exact ages at the end of this chapter but let me first offer you a framework for knowing when your particular child is ready.

Parents' roles: In a nutshell, here are the roles parents need to take to ensure that their children's experiences online are safe and beneficial: **make them earn** the privilege to use technologies, **educate** them at every step of the way about each new device, **make clear agreements** with their input, **monitor** their usage, **hold them accountable** to the agreements, and **connect with their friend's parents** to create a united front. Let me give specifics about each of these roles, starting with them earning the right to try the next new level of technology.

How Kids Can *Earn* the Right to Try New Technologies

Readiness for technology signs: First and foremost, your child needs to have proven to you with her behavior and actions over time that she is ready to handle each step of technology. Being able to have a cell phone and getting on social media sites is a privilege, not a right. And I think children should earn this opportunity. I'm breaking down how kids can earn new freedoms and privileges into four categories: social readiness, emotional readiness, their ability to keep their power, and their level of self-responsibility. The following are specific, concrete behaviors kids can develop to be ready.

Socially

- Stay disengaged from drama, not add to it, and do not allow herself to get sucked into the middle of friends' conflicts
- Handle conflicts directly, peacefully and effectively
- History of surrounding herself with healthy friends
- History of keeping herself in balance with schoolwork, activities, family time, dating partners, and taking breaks from friends when needed
- Social signs she may not be ready: has she struggled to make or keep friends? Is she currently being bullied, or has she been in the past? Is she being excluded? Does she lack a best friend or a group? Does she have a history of victimization? Has she been a target?

Emotionally

- Controls her emotions; able to catch herself, self-regulate, and think things through before she reacts
- Not let her buttons be pushed and overreact
- Does she suffer from anxiety, depression, or self-harm?
- Practices regular self-care
- Has the maturity and tools to express her emotions in healthy ways
- Takes quiet time to reflect and process experiences, emotions and thoughts so they don't build up to the point of overwhelm

Is she able to keep her power?
- Not allow words/rumors to hurt her
- Asks for what she wants, advocates for herself
- Not worry about what others think or let judgments affect her
- Not give up herself to fit in or to be accepted.
- Able to set clear, firm boundaries
- Make decisions different than friends, i.e., Have her own mind
- Not compare herself to the point of making herself anxious or depressed
- Image and media savvy

Self-responsible
- Keeps life in balance: school, friends, dating partner, family, job, self-care; has a variety of interests
- Gets enough sleep and has good sleep routines
- Handled previous levels of technology: tv, video games, tablets
- Has good impulse control; no addictive behaviors
- Makes good choices and decisions
- Learns from mistakes
- Track record of handling boredom
- Shares enough so that parents know how she thinks about important issues
- Transparent and willing to have heart-to-heart conversations with parents
- Follows agreements vs. Engaging in power struggles or rebelling
- Takes accountability for her actions

I know, I know, I know! That is a formidable list that many of *us* would have a hard time living up to. And no teenager is perfect. But, this is the blueprint you can give your kids starting in middle school to let them know that these are the important signs you will be looking for to know they are ready to have a phone or get on social media. Let me explain why these points are so important.

Growing Socially

A teen girl was out of shape at five feet, three inches tall and 172 lbs. After she had a minor accident, her mother accompanied her to the hospital emergency room. The admitting nurse asked for her height and weight, and she blurted out, "Five-foot-eight, 115 pounds." The nurse pondered over this information and looked over the patient. Then the girl's mother leaned over her daughter and gently chided, "Sweetheart, this is not the Internet."

Most friendship dramas that kids get entangled in start in person: in the hallways of school, in the lunchroom, in class, during soccer practice, on bus rides or at sleepovers. Social media magnifies, mirrors and makes more visible what occurs in real time and in real life: the good, the bad and the ugly. If you don't have the skills to handle conflicts directly and effectively, there's a good chance they will be brought online where people you do and don't know will weigh in and blow it up. If you feel left out, isolated, and lonely in person, you are vulnerable to getting overwhelmed by seeing your peers having fun at sleepovers or football games. Those sightings will reinforce your beliefs that you are unimportant, weird, socially awkward, not good enough or pretty enough or cool enough. Lonely girls I counsel are also more vulnerable to making errors in judgment about talking to strangers online.

My work for the past 15 years has exclusively been with girls in my counseling practice, retreats and summer camps. So, I am particularly sensitive to their social lives and challenges. Kids need to learn social-emotional awareness and skills that would allow them to pull off my list of social readiness proficiencies. Most of these can be learned and practiced at home, but some need to be addressed in groups with their peers. That's one of the main reasons I started my retreats and summer camps 35 years ago. If they can learn to deal with friendship issues in person then they will be more protected and mature online.

Growing emotionally: Having the emotional maturity to not allow other's words or judgments hurt you makes kids much less vulnerable to the dark side of social media. Having healthy outlets for your emotions prevents their build-up to symptoms of anxiety and depression. With emotional maturity comes the ability to think before you act/react and, thus, prevent unnecessary conflicts and relationship aggressions.

Growth in keeping your power: Becoming more inward-directed allows kids to be less affected by the dramas that swirl around them. Setting clear, firm boundaries with friends allows those relationships to become deeper and more trustworthy. And having close friends helps protect youth from being targeted for abuse. Social media will inundate users with messages about how they should look, feel, act and show up, so being centered and self-confident in who you are is the best insulation to combat those messages.

Becoming more self-responsible: I tell teens all the time that one of the best strategies for getting their folks to stop micromanaging them is to take responsibility for maintaining a healthy, balanced life. If they put in a reasonable effort with schoolwork and attain reasonable grades, spend time with their family so parents feel connected to them, take care of their bodies with adequate exercise, nutrition and sleep, and have enough face-to-face time with friends, then parents don't need to worry so much if they are on their phones for several hours a day. If they are out of balance in these important areas then they are asking their parents to get involved and take charge of their lives. Having demonstrated good impulse control and following through with boundaries with previous privileges and technologies shows parents they are ready to try the next level.

You can start teaching kids in grade school that they will be expected to earn any new privilege and freedom with prescribed behaviors over time. So, there won't always be an exact age when they will be allowed a new freedom; it will be granted when they have earned it. This is actually a good thing for kids because it puts the ball in their court. I encourage you to use directives such as: *"As soon as you show us A and B, we'll know you are ready for C." "Here's what we need to see from you that will tell us you are ready for___."* This was an invaluable process we used with our three children, and it's a process they will experience throughout their lives in earning the trust of teachers, coaches and employers.

Educate: Before receiving a phone or being allowed to get on new sites, parents should provide their children with a lot of education about online civility, ethics, and what is and is not appropriate. I would go through sites and inform each other about what restrictions parents have. Discuss things that are not suitable to say or display, including issues involving friendship conflicts and dramas. As tech-savvy as they may be, don't assume they have the maturity and knowledge that you possess. Three young adult women I recently interviewed for my podcast all described how they fell prey to images on social media, assuming they were reality. In the heat of the moment, preteens and teens can forget that social media increases the visibility of drama, enlarges the audience, and allows your interpersonal conflicts to be publicized to all. It makes your relationship dramas more visible to more people.

Here are two good analogies I use with girls to bring home these concerns.

First, I ask kids if they would be okay with me creating a large poster and writing down all the negative, snarky comments they've said to friends about other people they are mad at. And also putting naked photos of themselves on this poster as well. And finally, would it be okay if I placed this poster at the entrance to the airport so that everyone from all over the planet entering the airport would see it. "Of course not," they proclaim. I tell them that any time they post ANYTHING online they are at risk of it traveling globally without their permission.

A second analogy goes like this, in particular for girls who are being pressured by guys to send nudes. I ask if they'd want to not only strip down naked in front of their boyfriend but also allow him to invite all his friends over for the viewing. "Of course not!" they shout. Once again, any photos they post can develop legs and be passed throughout their school, their community and beyond.

Before getting onto sites, kids need to learn to critically evaluate posts and photos, see through biases and what's not real, and increase their digital wisdom. Help them become more image savvy by going on websites that show before and after photos of famous people and regular teens. See and understand all the ways photos are doctored to change the image. They can learn to remind themselves that every photo viewed online is probably not the original and has been changed. Thus, they don't need to compare themselves unfavorably to online pictures of peers or celebrities because they don't look that way normally either.

You can't educate them enough about these issues. If you read or hear a news report about someone who receives a negative repercussion for present or past postings, copy it and put it on your child's bed or discuss it with them the next time you take a walk. People have lost admittance to college, lost jobs or not been hired due to such transgressions.

Dad texts his son at college on a cold winter AM; "Windows frozen, won't open". Son texts back, "Gently pour some lukewarm water over it and then gently tap edges with a hammer." Dad texts back 10 minutes later, "Computer really messed up now."

I also advise you, Mom and Dad, to continue to educate yourselves about new technologies, social media platforms and online games. There is a constant infusion of the latest new thing that attracts the attention of kids. Stay on top of it. Oftentimes, the best teachers of what's new and hot are your children. Pull up a chair to their desk and have them give you tutorials. This includes them educating you about their understanding of what's real and what's not, and what is appropriate and what's not.

Also, know that no matter how hard you try to keep up with your kids and their devices, it's tough to keep up, as this dad found out. *"My daughter was wearing a flannel hoodie, so I said "Hey, the 90s called," and she replied, "Yeah, 'cause they couldn't text."* Sometimes you just can't win.

Agreements: Make specific, clear agreements about usage: the amount of screen and technology time allowed, what sites are okay to be on, who is appropriate for them to be connecting with online, and where and when they will park their gadgets at bedtime, so they are not on them all night. I would be sure that these are open conversations, with a lot of give and take, so that your children feel like they have been heard and their needs have been met as well as yours. And I would be clear that their online behavior and willingness to follow the agreements will decide their technology usage going forward.

Monitor: Let your children know up front that you will intermittently monitor their sites and texts, in essence, "spying openly." Tell them you won't check every day and each message, but you will go onto their devices and sites periodically to make sure they are using them correctly and following your agreements. It's no different than going downstairs periodically during a party your adolescent throws just to have a presence. You are making sure they are safe at a time when they need boundaries. In essence, you perform the duties of a mature prefrontal cortex that has yet to mature in them. But also remember the points I made in chapter 11 about kids and teens today lacking the freedoms and unsupervised time as we did. They need room to breathe, stretch their decision-making muscles, and earn more trust. Tell your kids that if they earn a good track record of being appropriate online and following agreements, you will begin easing off monitoring.

On the other hand, if your child starts showing signs that they aren't okay, such as being depressed or anxious, having a hard time adjusting to major life changes, not demonstrating good coping skills, or becoming isolated and lonely, then you are going to step in and help them figure out how to get back on track. This becomes less a technology issue and more of a mental health concern. For example, teens who engage in risky online behaviors or experience internet-initiated sexual assaults are rare. These tend to occur with teens who have more problems offline that need to be addressed.

I believe it's critical to monitor more in the early period of your child's usage until you see that they have the maturity and awareness of digital right and wrong. But I also commiserate with young adults whose parents are still monitoring them with the 360 app even when they are in college. I heard about a mom who one day was complaining about her daughter. *Mom: "My daughter thinks I'm way too nosey and in her business, or at least that's what she keeps writing in her diary."* Don't be that mom!

Follow Through

"I asked my son to turn down his music, and he 'okay boomer'd' me, so now we're turning off the wi-fi for a bit."

Too many parents fall short in holding their children accountable to the agreements. If you find that your child has broken the contract, I would have a heart-to-heart talk about why they didn't follow through with the agreement and what they will do to avoid the same error next time. There are good reasons why teens make mistakes online, usually having to do with a lack of skills, worrying too much about losing friends, FOMO (fear of missing out), and lacking the courage to handle friendship issues. They are also at ages where making and keeping friends is of vital importance. I'd commiserate about how hard it is to have different rules than their friends or to think before they act.

What do you do when your child makes a mistake or doesn't follow your agreement? Use these slip-ups as opportunities to listen, understand, empathize, educate and build skills. There's always a reason why kids butt up against a decision point where they sense their internal alarm, intuition or conscience go off but then choose to ignore it. Help them become aware of the reason why they ignored the alarm, and then what they will do so they are not so vulnerable next time they face that choice point. If missteps are repeated, then they have shown you that they aren't ready for that level of technology. They need time to mature, become more responsible and less impulsive, and develop more skills. Once they have shown you over time, i.e., months, that they have gained this new wisdom, maturity and reliability, you can try it again.

Friend's parents: Talk with the parents of your children's good friends so that you have a united front. Have everyone over for a BBQ and discuss the issue of when to allow kids their 1st phone and social media. Every parent I've met is worried about this issue. Perhaps make a group agreement about starting ages so that you are all on the same page. Then, when your daughter complains that "All of my friends have a phone," you can look her in the eye and remind her that all of her best friends actually don't. It's nice to have that kind of support. And a good working relationship with your child's teachers will make it easier to handle any out-of-school online situations in partnership with the school.

At the start of this chapter I promised I'd give you the exact best ages to allow kids to get their 1st phone and be allowed on social media. What my wife and I have been saying to parents for the past 15 years is that we don't think kids are ready for their 1st smartphone until 8th or 9th grade, and for social media, not until they are in 9th-10th grade. And both of those ages has the add-on stipulation that they also must have shown enough readiness signs to have earned the privilege. In my experience, it's more of a readiness issue than it is an exact age. The middle school years are the stage where kids are most insecure, sensitive, impulsive and overly concerned with what others think. Your child might be mature but the context they swim in every day is hard to maneuver in. That's why I think high school is a good cutoff point.

BTW, don't forget about the value of a full goodwill account with your child. Having a close relationship allows you to have meaningful conversations, create real win-win agreements, and hold your child accountable to the agreements you've made.

Remember, too, that because we have shrunken kids' geographic freedom, we have, in essence, forced them to hang out online. This became increasingly true during our pandemic isolation. Social networking sites often are the only public spaces to get together with some measure of privacy and autonomy. Your kids use social media to understand the social mores of their peer group, figure out where they stand in the group, and understand their social currency and power and place in the hierarchy. Just like we did, kids and teens need to learn street smarts and manage friendships and their social lives to develop independence, self-reliance, social skills and resilience.

As I wind down this chapter, let me offer some random thoughts and poignant phrases that encapsulate the good, the bad, and the ugly of our technologies. I'll put the names of my favorite books on this topic in the bibliography, with special mention to authors Sherry Turkle, William Powers, Danah Boyd, Jonathon Haidt and Kelly McGonigal. And most importantly, I've learned so much from listening to girls in my counseling practice, high school support groups, and sitting in circles on the floor at my weekend retreats and summer camps as girls shared their stories, feelings, needs and desires, and their adversities.

One of the main results of relating online is that you are there but not there, always reachable, and experiencing companionship with convenience. Every person becomes pauseable, and we rarely have anyone's full attention. We end up with intimacy without privacy, and a new belief that convenience and control in relationships are more valued than commitment and closeness. Online communication feels more like ties that preoccupy vs. ties that bind.

Despite the many hours kids and teens spend online, their generation feels lonelier than past ones. Author Sherry Turkle, in her book *Reclaiming Conversation*, wrote that loneliness is failed solitude. I have found teens and young adults today lack the ability to get quiet, be alone, and experience solitude, reflection, deliberateness and slowness. One of the main costs is that they have not learned who they are, what makes them tick, what they need, or what is their purpose and calling. They seem younger and more lost than in previous generations.

Online friends become followers and fans vs. true friends. Research has found a decrease in college students' interest in other people in the past 30 years, including a 40% decrease in their empathy since 1980. This doesn't surprise me a bit.

Trauma from 9-11 heightened parents' fears about their children. We kept hearing stories of people cut off from loved ones, causing us to feel terrorized right along with those in New York. As a result, cell phones became a symbol of parental security and emotional safety. Parents ever since have needed the comfort of continuous contact with their kids. Kids, in turn, learned that you need your phone to feel safe and that they must have constant connection with home.

Since parents are always just a text away, kids rely more on them than themselves to solve problems. It is normal to feel confusion, self-doubt and angst in situations that require you to solve problems, take action, and work through the normal ups and downs of growing up. We've conditioned our kids to rely too much on externals to guide them, including us. We've normalized college students calling home every day or even several times a day. And most seemed resigned to the fact that their parent wants to follow them 24/7 on apps like 360 to be sure they are safe. Even for 20-somethings, parents can always find them and check up on them. It's a different world, my friends. Young adults and parents in past generations would have laughed at the thought of that kind of micromanagement.

There is another huge cost for kids to be plugged in constantly: they become outwardly focused and never hear from themselves. Girls I work with who are continually online sending and receiving texts and checking sites like Instagram over and over again haven't heard from themselves in a long, long time. It's impossible to feel grounded and centered living this way.

Compared with boys, when girls go onto social media, they are subjected to more severe and constant judgments about their looks and their bodies, and they're confronted with beauty standards that are unrealistic and unattainable. This pressure to look good causes girls to obsess over how they put themselves out there and increases the pressure to fit in and to fit unhealthy stereotypes and social mores. It's hard to be grounded when you are constantly experiencing this new kind of performance anxiety.

As soon as teenagers began carrying smartphones to school and using social media regularly, including during breaks between classes and even at the lunch table, it became harder to connect with their fellow students. Healthy social development requires synchronous, face-to-face communication. Without it, kids and teens report feeling socially awkward, lonely and isolated. Girls tell me that even in a group of their "good friends" they often feel isolated. College women tell me that it's hard to make new friends because everyone is walking around campus with their heads down, looking at their phones. Jonathon Haidt describes how Gen Z became the first generation in history to go through puberty with a communication device in their pockets that called them away from people nearby and into an alternative universe that was exciting, addictive, unstable, and improper for kids and adolescents.

As I've described in chapter 11, we are overprotecting kids as far as going outside and having freedom with friends and restricting their autonomy in the real world while, at the same time, under protecting them online, where they are particularly vulnerable during adolescence. Kids subsequently become more anxious, less confident and competent, less able to cope with adversities life throws at them, and much less grounded and sure of themselves.

Finally, despite all of this information and these reflections, remember that you are not powerless! Take charge, stay on top of new technology, keep your goodwill account full, and follow through with the agreements you make with your child.

Chapter 15

Self-Quieting

We've done a fabulous job in our culture of teaching kids how to be busy, distracted and overcommitted. Where we are failing is teaching children how to be quiet and still and to be alone with themselves. This chapter will offer ideas about how to teach kids the value of self-quieting and mindfulness and the skills to accomplish it.

I see more and more kids and teenagers today at younger and younger ages experiencing problems with anxiety, worrying, an inability to fall asleep at night time, and complaining of being "stressed out." Like the adults around them, kids are go-go-go all day long with school, sports, activities and homework. Mixed into this busyness is far too little family time. And then there are the hours spent glued to their screens, communicating with friends and endlessly scrolling social media walls. All of this activity makes for a busy, noisy, distracting day and evening with little or no down time.

With so much focus on achievement and success, we have lost sight of core values like solitude, reflection, soul searching, daydreaming, contemplation and questioning. You need to be quiet and still to accomplish the above. It saddens and worries me that we don't value these skills anymore.

So it's no wonder that when kids, especially teens, finally turn the lights out and lay down to fall asleep, they have a hard time shutting it all down. It's the only time all day that they are alone and quiet. And so up comes all of the thoughts, worries, and feelings that they have stuffed, stored up, and distracted themselves from all day long. The quietness is deafening, and it becomes overwhelming for many kids and teens (and adults too).

This is the only time of the day that they actually are in touch with their feelings, the only time they are quiet enough without all the distractions to allow feelings to emerge. It is these emotions and thoughts bubbling to the surface that prevent kids from settling down and falling to sleep.

A child's temperament can also contribute to an extra need for quieting. This is true for kids who, by nature, are intense, perfectionists, particular, anxious, worriers, brooders, ruminate a lot or are physically active. It's also true for kids who have a hard time letting things go, have a low frustration tolerance, internalize feelings vs. expressing them, are sensitive to external stimuli such as lights, noise, clothes or crowds, or who are sensitive emotionally and get their feelings hurt easily. This is also true for many of the girls I counsel, who are extremely empathetic and deep, and who absorb the feelings of all those around them.

There are also certain developmental/behavioral stages where quiet, alone time becomes more important and necessary. This is especially true during stages where kids go through periods of growing up emotionally (middle school years, during puberty, eighteen-year-old high school seniors). During these stages, they are restless, moody, out of sorts, and tend to be more reactive. My old mentor, Dr. Berry Brazelton, called these predictable times touch points. Just before and during the transition to a new stage of development, kids tend to fall apart until they reach the new level. Then there is a period of homeostasis that lasts until the next touch point, and the process repeats. The restlessness during the waking hours tends to carry over to nighttime, so kids have a harder time falling asleep, staying asleep, and sleeping soundly. The decrease in sleep causes kids to be more irritable during the day, and the cycle feeds on itself.

The busyness in the child's life can also contribute to kids feeling more unsettled and overwhelmed. This might include:

schoolwork pressures and intense extracurricular activities such as club sports, plays, auditions, competitive cheerleading, etc. It may include long work hours after school and during evenings, transitional years to middle school, high school, or college, changing schools, or moving. It's easy and common for kids to feel overwhelmed from being out of balance with all of the above.

The stress can also come from more personal experiences that could include: parental discord, separations or divorce, deaths, any family stress such as job changes, financial worries, problems with relatives, time spent with aging grandparents (sandwich generation), disabilities, parental mental health problems, or family concerns about a sibling's mental, physical, emotional or academic health. Stress and overload can also develop from an unsafe home and neighborhood, parents placing undue pressure and excessively high expectations on kids, and parents who use a critical, judgmental, physical, punitive and authoritative parenting style.

And finally, kids really do tend to reflect the adult world around them. If there is tension, anger and distance between parents, kids in some way will reflect that behaviorally and react against it. Really deep and sensitive kids will also react against what is happening in the world as well. Hurricanes, wars, and stories about kidnappings and home break-ins can cause these types of kids to be anxious, worried, extra clingy and insecure, and have sleeping problems. These sensitive kids can also tell when a parent is depressed, anxious, distant or distracted, and in some way, they will reflect this with their mood and behavior.

Did I mention how noisy, distracting and busy the culture is just in general? There is so much noise and visual overload from so many ads, cell phones, video games and streaming content. It seems that we are constantly being bombarded with sights, sounds, advertising and fear-mongering no matter where you turn.

So, how can you keep your kids grounded and peaceful amidst all of this hustle, bustle, stimulation and stress? What follows are suggestions that look at self-quieting as a long-term learning process, which starts in utero and proceeds throughout the teen years. I say in utero because of seeing many babies on ultrasound sucking their fingers and thumbs, already experts at self-soothing.

The long-term self-quieting process is easy to lay out but harder to implement. Your intention for your child is that they will learn to become aware of their body signals that tell them they are beginning to get restless and dysregulated and that they are starting down the path of no return, if you will. This awareness from experience tells them, "If I don't do something now, I will get myself worked up to the point that nothing works well."

Let me share a good analogy I have used for years in my counseling practice, retreats and camps about learning to regulate your emotions. I had this exact conversation with a 7-year-old girl recently who regularly lost it with her parents.

Me: If you put a pot of water on the stove, what does it look like when the dial is at zero?

Sally: "It's calm and still."

Me: "What do you look like when you are at a zero level and calm?"

Sally: "My body is calm and quiet. I talk in my normal voice."

Me: If you turn the heat up to 4-5, then what happens to the water? It starts to steam a little and then begins to bubble. What do you look/act like when you start to bubble?

Sally: "My body starts to feel tense, my hands clench, my jaw gets tight, and my voice is louder and a little angry."

Me: If you turn the heat back down to zero, it doesn't take very long for the water to calm; same goes for your feelings. What happens to the water if I turn the heat up to levels 7-8? It starts to bubble, then it begins to boil. What are you like at a 7-8?

Sally: "I get angry, I start to yell and stomp around, I may say disrespectful things."

Me: If you turn the dial down to zero, it takes longer for the water to get calm, just like your emotions. What happens if I then turn the dial all the way up to 10? The water bubbles, then starts to boil until it spills over the top and makes a mess. What happens to you when you are at a 10?

Sally: "I get more and more angry; I stop listening to everyone; I yell and stomp and throw things. I say mean things to people like I hate you and may even break things."

Me: If you turn the dial back to zero, it can take a long time to settle back down, maybe as long as 30-60 minutes.

Using this analogy, kids can learn to catch themselves when they start to bubble, recognizing that they are starting to go down the path of no return. They can then learn to remove themselves from the situation, go someplace and do their self-quieting skills until they are calmed down, regulated and grounded. And then they can return to the dinner table, classroom, soccer game (or board meeting someday). When kids, or adults for that matter, become dysregulated, i.e., become frustrated, angry or ready to explode, the emotional part of their brains operates at full speed ahead. When that happens, the executive center of the brain, the prefrontal cortex (PFC), shuts down. That part of the brain helps us to calm down, reason through frustrations or triggers, think before we act, and access memories to give us a perspective that we've been here before and it's not that big of a deal. But the PFC won't be able to regulate our emotions until the emotional centers calm down. That is where mindfulness and self-quieting skills come into play.

At first, parents will need to help kids become aware of when they are starting to lose it because we will notice their symptoms before they are aware of them. I ask kids if their parents have permission to come to them and say that they can tell you are starting to bubble and then to have them check in with themselves. Ask her questions like, "Can you tell right now that you are starting to bubble? Where do you feel it in your body? How do you experience it? What's going on in your head?"

If you catch kids early on, they are more willing and able to check in with themselves and discuss it. You'll hear answers like: "My hands are sweaty. My chest is getting tight. I have butterflies in my stomach. I feel busy inside. I have lots of thoughts in my head that I can't stop."

Eventually, they will be able to catch themselves as they are getting restless, angry or stressed and remove themselves. That's the long-term goal.

You also must give kids some self-calming tools to use when they need them. Look at their history to get clues about what might work best for them. What has helped in the past to calm them down? Are they into drawing? Reading? Writing? Music? Are they more visual, auditory or kinesthetic? Do they play an instrument? Do they like to write poetry or stories? Are they more physical?

The following list contains examples of many different ways of self-quieting, with the earlier items for younger kids and advancing down the list with ideas for older kids and teens.

Ways for Children to Self-Calm

1. Coloring.
2. Playdough.
3. Listening to a book-on-tape.
4. Listen to a tape with their parent's voice reading some calming stories or guided imagery stories.

5. Physical outlets - shoot baskets or pucks, kick a soccer ball, take a walk. Any kind of rhythmic activity—like being rocked or jumping on a trampoline or even walking—does an amazing job of quieting anyone, from babies through adults.
6. Zen garden, lava lamp, kaleidoscope.
7. Talk to pets/stuffed animals.
8. Quiet time in your safe space.
9. Read a book.
10. Express your feelings through drawings, painting, or coloring.
11. Write fictional stories about a girl your age going through what you are, how she feels and how she manages the adversity
12. Write poetry expressing how you feel.
13. Write in a journal or diary.
14. Write a letter expressing your feelings, then rip it up.
15. Write a song.
16. Play an instrument (guitar, piano, drums, etc.).
17. Listening to music confers the rhythmic calm similar to being rocked
18. Repeat a mantra.
19. Relaxation tapes.
20. Breathwork tapes.
21. Guided imagery tapes.
22. Quiet time in nature.

23. Talk to someone about how you are feeling, i.e. parents, friend, counselor, teacher
24. Meditate daily.

The idea is that you make this process like a treasure hunt, trying to learn what works for your child. Trial and error work best, guided by your previous observations of your child. If kids feel that you care and that you are a supportive partner in this learning process, you should get good cooperation from them.

The value for kids in learning this process is manyfold. First and foremost, it is empowering and feels good to know you can take care of yourself and your emotions. Self-quieting is also an essential balance to all the busyness we experience. Kids can fall asleep quicker and sleep more soundly.

Kids also learn how to check in with themselves, and in particular, to check in with how they are feeling. You can't do that when you are busy and distracted. In their quiet times, they can express their emotions in effective ways by journaling, writing stories, poetry, drawing, writing songs, etc. Being connected to your emotions and being able to express them regularly allows kids to feel more calm, peaceful and grounded.

Many of the preteens and teenagers I see in my counseling practice come to me with diagnoses like anxiety disorder or depression. What I have found over the years is that most of them don't deserve a diagnosis or medications. Their behaviors are symptoms of being overloaded. They don't like to think about or feel the emotions and thoughts about their adverse experiences, so they get busy or distract themselves from them. It works in the moment, but these feelings don't go away for good; they tend to build to the point of overwhelm. They then leak out as symptoms such as: having a hard time falling or staying asleep, somatic complaints such as stomachaches or headaches, snapping at those around them or at themselves with negative self-talk, anxiety, feeling blah and losing their motivation, or being distracted. I encourage them to have a regular time where they can express their thoughts and feelings to lessen the pile and prevent the buildup.

Teenagers also need time to think, reflect and soul search. There are so many questions to find answers for including: "Who am I? What's my dream? What's my purpose for being on this planet? Which high school or college is right for me? How far do I want to go sexually? Should I get high? What am I feeling inside? Am I happy with how I look? Can I trust myself?"

The answers to these types of important questions are best found within us. To get these answers, to hear our inner voice, we must learn to become silent. Validation and motivation need to come from within too. Instead of looking to your peers, the media or the culture, I want teens to look inside themselves for their validation and direction.

Remember too, as described in chapter 7, about the value of spending time in nature. Nature provides places for healing, reflection, quieting and getting "grounded."

Be patient with teaching your kids this process; keep remembering that they will use these tools for the rest of their lives. Discuss this process with them, honor their input and suggestions, get their buy-in, work out a plan about how you will implement it together, and get to work. Your child will feel understood and supported.

Together with your child, create a self-calming area in the house where everyone can go when they need to chill out and refuel. Some kids like to create a safe space in their room, where they can keep any materials/aids in one spot, i.e., drawing materials, music, books, journals, etc. Or it could be a more central spot in your family room. Be creative and listen to what works best for your kids and your family.

And finally, remember the importance of modeling. Let your kids see you catch yourself when getting angry or crabby, go to the self-quieting area and do your thing. Let them know by your words and example that you practice quieting skills too. Let them see you meditating, practicing yoga or journal writing.

Keeping yourself and your family feeling grounded is a tough challenge in this present culture. Stay committed to teaching this process no matter what and you and your children will reap the benefits now and forever. Let me leave you with one of my favorite poems by Shel Silverstein that relates to this topic: *Voice Inside of You: There is a voice inside of you, that whispers all day long, I feel that this is right for me, I know that this is wrong. No teacher, preacher, parent, friend or wise man can decide, What's right for you, just listen to, the voice that speaks inside.*

Chapter 16

Staying Connected with Your Teenager

"Having a teen is sending an 'I love you' text and getting back a thumbs-up reply."

Having teenagers in your home can bring much chaos and tension or much enrichment and enjoyment. The results depend upon parents' attitudes and their ability to stay disciplined.

Parenting a teenager is very much like parenting 18- to 36-month-olds who are going through their autonomy stage. There is no magical cure or consequence that will quickly stop toddlers from throwing temper tantrums or pushing limits. Our job as parents isn't to stop the behavior. Our job is to handle their boundary-pushing effectively and consistently so that over time, they "get it." By the time toddlers reach four years of age, they should be moving out of that stage if, and that's a big if, if parents have stayed detached from all the drama and maintained consistent, clear boundaries.

The same goes with teenagers. They are supposed to be moody; they are supposed to test boundaries and struggle for more freedom. It's not our job to stop this necessary developmental process. They need us to keep our emotions out of the mix, to not take their behaviors personally, to hold them accountable to agreements, and to stay connected with them in ever-changing ways.

When kids enter puberty, their brains begin a process of remodeling by pruning off unused neurons and growing new ones while strengthening connections between them. The posterior parts of the brain undergo remodeling first, and this includes their emotional centers (amygdala). This results in a well-developed amygdala but an immature prefrontal cortex (PFC). During puberty the brain first starts strengthening parts that allow them to feel intense and complex emotions; teenagers might rely on their amygdala to make decisions and solve problems more than adults do. The amygdala is associated with emotions, impulses, aggression and instinctive behavior.

However, the part of the brain that is responsible for regulating emotions, deep thinking, reasoning and decision making is often the last to develop (PFC), causing teens to feel out of control and overwhelmed.

I don't care how many degrees you have; nothing prepares you for a teen who finds their phone didn't charge overnight.

What you want to occur for teens is this: as they begin to get agitated when their amygdala starts firing, you want a message to get quickly sent to the PFC to regulate themselves. Unfortunately, in an immature brain, the impulses sent to the PFC are slow, causing the emotional upheavals common at this age. As they mature, their brains are better able to sift through information, reason, reflect, and pull from old memories to regulate their emotions. The immature teen brain uses the fast route, bypasses the cortex and simply sends streams of perception directly to the amygdala. Thus, teenagers don't think before they act; they behave impulsively, and their emotions override reason. If you've ever asked your teenager, "What were you thinking?" The answer is that they weren't. They were acting through their emotions, not their PFC. Full brain maturation isn't finished in girls until about age 18 to 20, and for males, it's mid-20s.

Most adults describe teens disapprovingly, seeing them as undisciplined, disrespectful, rude and unfriendly. Many adults are actually afraid of teenagers, lumping them together as being violent, angry, selfish and uncaring. This is described well by this parent: *Can anyone recommend a good wine that pairs well with a teenager's shitty attitude?* It's no wonder that teens today feel disconnected from their parents and other adults.

The Search Institute has published data about teenagers living in urban and suburban communities around the country. The following are the percent of teens responding positively to these community assets:

1. Young people and their parents communicate positively, and young people are willing to seek their parent's advice and counsel: 24%

2. Young people receive support from three or more non-parent adults: 41%

3. Young people experience caring neighbors: 34%

4. School provides a caring, encouraging environment: 27%

5. Parents are actively involved in helping young people succeed in school: 27%

6. Young people perceive that adults in the community value youth: 19%

7. Young people are given useful roles in the community: 28%

8. Parents and other adults model positive, responsible behavior: 28%

9. Young people feel safe at home, school, and in the neighborhood: 28%

Could there possibly be a more unappreciated, unloved, disconnected and underutilized group in our society? We wonder why so many teenagers today are hurting and angry. I'd like to lay forth for you my vision of how to reconnect with our teenagers, how to support our teens in staying grounded, and how we can best nurture our relationships with them even as we, too, are all flying by the seat of our pants. The following are ways we can meet their developmental, behavioral and emotional needs.

A Baker's Dozen Ways to Relate to Your Teenager

Respect their ideas and feelings

Be willing to get in their shoes and to see and understand the world from their point of view. The prayer of St. Francis holds the line, "Seek first to understand, then to be understood." This is especially true when relating to teenagers. You do not have to agree with them. Just be willing to get out of your world and into theirs to understand their perspective and validate their feelings.

Do not enter their room without their permission

Having a teenager is like having a cat that only comes out to eat and hisses when you try and pet it.

Teens need lots of private, quiet time to think, to get clear about life events and to talk to their friends. They need to feel safe enough to pour their hearts out into their journals, poetry, artwork and music without worrying that someone (like their parents) will be snooping around their room looking for their secrets. Past generations were able to hang out with friends without constant adult supervision outside of their homes. Teens today don't have that luxury.

Do not enter their relationships without their permission

They aren't privy to the nitty-gritty goings-on between you and your spouse or your friends, and they need this same kind of space with their relationships. Above all, never, ever, ever criticize or negatively judge their friends. In a sense, most teens feel like they are their friends. When you negatively judge their friends and you do not want to spend time with their friends, you are in their minds judging them and don't want to spend time with them.

It is nearly impossible for teens today to have the kind of privacy and freedoms we had growing up. We can periodically check on their digital conversations and photographs as well as their friend's. As described in chapter 11, kids and teens have lost the kind of geographic freedom their parents experienced because of our fears. They are tethered to us 24/7, forever reachable. And if a parent texts them, they expect an immediate reply or parents will call 911. Not really, but you get the picture. They need more privacy!

Respect their space

There are times when teens want to be with us, so at those times drop everything and run with it. Many times they do not want to be seen within ten miles of us, so respect that as well. Do not take it personally; it really is not about us. And perhaps follow the advice of Nora Ephron: *"When your children are teenagers, it's important to have a dog so that someone in the house is happy to see you."*

Give more control, power, and "say-so"

Research shows that the results of teens not getting enough say-so at home are decreased motivation, decreased school performance, increased anger and depression and more acting out. Listen to their needs a lot and give as much control as is reasonable to them (see chapter 9 on family meetings). They will learn more from their own successes and mistakes out in the world than they will from our lectures (see chapter 11).

Agreements and accountability vs. rules and consequences

Me: Will you empty the dishwasher, please? My teenager: I'm good. Me: Thank you. My teenager: That actually means No.... that's how my generation talks. Me: Let's try this again, Empty the fecking dishwasher or you'll get my foot up your arse, That's how MY generation talks, Fiona O'Brien #IrishMom

Create win-win agreements giving them a lot of say-so about how their life looks and operates. Be sure everyone is clear about the agreements and has bought in. Then be sure to follow through in a kind but firm way no matter what. Stay out of the business of making the rules, passing them down to your subjects (your teens) and then using punishments for motivation. It rarely works with teens and creates major unnecessary power struggles. (see chapter 10 on boundaries and discipline).

Have fun with them

One winter night, our then 16-year-old son, John had a bunch of his friends over to spend the night. After watching the St. Louis Rams lose a playoff football game, they asked me if I'd take them to see two of their friends play in a Varsity high school hockey game. It was 11 p.m.— the game started at 11:30, and I was tired, but I sucked it up and said sure, I'd take them.

It started snowing an hour earlier, but I packed six of them into my car, and off we went. As always, I shut my mouth and listened as I heard all the latest gossip about girls and teachers. They asked me if I'd brought any CDs, so I put in my Camp Weloki dance music mix.

That mix contains a lot of old dance songs from Backstreet Boys, Brittney Spears and the Spice Girls, which, for them, are "lame and stupid." But wouldn't you know it, within seconds, they were all screaming the lyrics and having a blast! They knew every word of every song, and for a few moments, they forgot about being cool and the little kid in them came out to play.

If I had said no to their request to go to the game, I would have missed out on a great time and a fantastic memory. So, when your teen opens that door into their world or their hearts, don't hesitate! Jump in and get reconnected and learn something about who they are and who they are becoming.

Walk your talk

A dad explains ethics to his daughter, who is about to go into business. "Suppose a woman comes in and orders $100 worth of material. You wrap it up and give it to her. She pays you with a $100 bill. As she leaves, you realize she's given you two $100 bills. Now, here's where the ethics come in. Should you, or should you not tell your partner?"

Hopefully, you'll do a better job of modeling integrity than this dad. There is little that riles up teenagers more than adults with double standards. If you do not want your 16-year-old drinking and driving, then do not have a glass of wine before you go out for the evening and drive. They are watching us like hawks. Practice what you preach. Be in integrity with whatever you are asking of them. It's a great way to show teenagers respect. I've never been much of a drinker, but when our kids were in grade school, I made it important to never have a drink, not even just a beer or a glass of wine, prior to driving. I wanted to be able to look them in the eyes when they were sixteen and driving and remind them that they had NEVER seen me drink and drive, not even one beer. I was on firm ground in those moments.

Respect and love yourself

They learn best how to take care of themselves by watching how we take care of ourselves. How well is your life balanced? Are you putting your heart and soul into work that you love? Do you eat healthy and exercise regularly? Do you nurture your friendships? Do you take time for spiritual growth?

Respect and love your spouse

Again, as they embark on the journey of learning about and experiencing special, close intimate relationships, they will lean heavily upon what they have seen at home. Have you shown them peaceful conflict resolution? Do they see a fun and affectionate relationship? Is there cooperation and mutual respect? Do you give of yourself but also not lose yourself in the relationship? Are there kind but firm boundaries in your marriage? Have they seen a committed, loving, respectful relationship that grows over time? They deserve to have experienced all of this and more. Your marriage is the most important template they will draw from when it comes to their own relationships.

You reap what you sow

If you want more respect from your teen, give them more respect. Whatever you are demanding of them, first be sure you are giving it in abundance. That goes for love, time, respect, or trust. You can take responsibility for any lack of love or respect in your relationship with your teen by giving it to them unconditionally tenfold. That goes against some of our old paradigms, but you truly will reap what you sow with teenagers.

Love and accept them for exactly who they are

Honor their differences. See through their exteriors (pink hair, baggy pants, ear and nose piercings) and do not judge a book by its cover. Beneath all the 'stuff' is the same cuddly, warm, funny little kid you used to wrestle with and hold on your lap just a few short years back. There is still a lot of "little kid" in our teens. Make it safe enough for those funny, playful, vulnerable parts of them to come out and play.

Teenagers in our culture are judged so negatively today without most adults ever taking the time to get to know them. Smile at them, look for their unique spirit. Let them know that you believe in them and their future despite some "bumps in the road" and some rough, growing edges during their teen years. A 1982 study of 160,000 high school seniors asked the question, "What do you want most in life?" The overwhelming number one response was,

"I just want to be loved." Love them unconditionally. This true story written by John Kord Lagemann demonstrates this perfectly.

A university professor sent his students out into a Baltimore slum to interview two hundred boys and then predict their chances for a successful future. The students were shocked at the poor conditions the boys came from and thus predicted that 90% of the boys would someday spend time in prison. Twenty-five years later, the same professor sent another class to find out how the predictions turned out.

Of the original 190 boys interviewed, only four had been imprisoned. How had these boys overcome their adverse conditions? More than 100 of them remembered one high school teacher, a Miss O'Rourke, as having been an inspiration in their lives. After a long search, Sheila O'Rourke was found. When asked to explain her influence over her former students, she was puzzled. "All I can say," she finally decided, "is that I loved every one of them."

Have fun

Let the awkward, spontaneous, goofy, funny, idealistic, adventurous teen come out in you. I sometimes wonder if the world wouldn't be better off if it was run by teenagers. They have such fresh, idealistic energy. Think of all their high, fun, culture-altering energy demonstrated by phenomena like Beatlemania and today's Taylor Swift craziness. Enjoy the ride with your teen. You'll never have one like it again!

The most important factor in how much cooperation and how much influence you have with your teens is the state of your relationship with them, i.e., your Goodwill Account (See chapter 4). If you have taken the time to invest in the relationship and the goodwill account is full, then it is easy to sit down and work out win-win agreements and then follow through. You can have a positive influence on their lives because they will not be afraid to come to you and use you to brainstorm or to be a sounding board. They will trust you have understanding ears. They will be in a space to listen to some of your wisdom and experience.

Despite their sometimes surly or "I don't care" external appearance, teens do need us. Perhaps they need us more than ever before in their lives. But our involvement must look different than previously.

It is important to use the "Baker's Dozen" list at times when everyone seems so rushed and stressed out. Do not forget about the special needs of your teenagers and the distinct skills needed to stay connected to them. Let us work together to change the current feelings that teenagers are awful and that, during those teen years, parents and teens must separate and dislike each other. Do not buy into the theory that you should be disconnected until some magical moment in their 20s. Both teenagers and their parents want closeness and love from each other, so work at it. I'd encourage you to continually ask your child all along the way how they want to be supported now at this age. I also encourage teens to be honest about what feels supportive vs. what feels annoying or constraining. Be patient and understanding when you experience something like this Mom: *My daughter went back to college today, and I texted her that I missed her so much, and she texted back 2.5 hours later, "Yes." Then, "Sorry, that wasn't for you."* Once again, enjoy the ride; it goes fast.

Chapter 17

Taking Care of Yourself and Your Marriage

Several years ago, at one of our summer camps, we were having some struggles with three girls, all around nine years of age. They just couldn't stop annoying each other. As soon as one of them would build a sandcastle at the lake, the other one would come and kick it over.

We worked with them on peaceful conflict resolution skills all to no avail. Every day in our course room "learning time," we worked with the entire kids' camp on skills for making friends, setting good boundaries, handling their disagreements and asking for what they needed. Usually after a few days at our camps, kids have really bonded and become very sensitive to each other's needs and are very inclusive. But not these three girls.

By the fourth day, some of our staff were becoming frustrated with the girl's mischief, so after our barbeque dinner at the dock, we had the campers swim at the lake with the lifeguards while the staff circled up to share and vent. And vent, we did!

At first, a lot of the comments were pointed at the three kids, blaming them for the mischief they were into. But then the focus shifted to where it really needed to shift— to ourselves.

I asked our staff, "How are we doing?" "Is everyone feeling okay about the staff?" "Is anyone not feeling included or valuable or heard?" "Is there anything we need to handle with each other?"

We all looked around the circle and shrugged our shoulders as if to say, "It's not us, we're all fine." But then someone said that they had been feeling a little distant from one of the staff because of something they had said a few days back. They hadn't said anything because they didn't want to make any waves, but could they handle it now?

So, they did what we'd been asking our campers to do all week, i.e., handle their conflict in a peaceful, productive way. Several other counselors followed suit and handled some small but important grievances until we all felt complete as a staff. We then made commitments to each other to handle any future issues quickly before they festered into discord and distance. With renewed energy and heightened spirits, we rejoined the kids.

And wouldn't you know it, for the rest of the week we didn't have any more problems with those three girls or the rest of the campers as well! No more conflicts and anger. And we didn't say a word to the kids about our staff meeting. How did this happen?

Kids are always a reflection of the adults around them, be it parents in the home, teachers at school or camp counselors at camp. If parents are peaceful, calm, patient, and present, kids will sense that, and it will be reflected in their behavior; kids will be more calm, patient and peaceful.

If, on the other hand, parents are tired, crabby, impatient, distant and angry, that too will be reflected in kids, as they will tend to be more angry, intolerant and into more fighting, conflicts and mischief.

Kids also are sensitive to the state of their parents' relationship. If there is a lot of tension, anger and distance in the marriage, kids will, in some way, usually negatively, reflect that in their behavior. If parents are close, loving, kind and affectionate towards each other, that too will be reflected in children's behavior in positive ways.

If there is a lot of chaos and anger in your home, such as sibling conflicts and fighting or a lot of disrespect and poor cooperation, instead of pointing your finger at your kids and blaming them, I'd suggest you first take a good, hard and honest look at yourself and your marriage. Check in with yourself: "Have I been happy, relaxed and focused on the kids when I've been with them? Have I been patient and present? Or have I been distracted, tired, impatient, crabby and distant, or not fully present?'

Then, check in with your marriage and ask similar questions. If the answers aren't positive, then start there within yourself and within your marriage. Clean up those areas first and handle your feelings and your mischief. And you will immediately see changes with your kids.

This leads me to the title of this very important chapter, "Taking Care of Yourself." It is so easy, especially if you are a first-time parent or the parent of young children, to put everyone and everything ahead of taking care of yourself. That is a huge mistake! Because taking care of you and your marriage creates the foundation from which everything will flow in your home.

Remember the analogy about the oxygen masks on airplanes? The stewardess always says, "In case of an emergency, the oxygen masks will come down. If you are traveling with young children, put your own mask on first and then help your child put theirs on." Take care of yourself first or you'll be worthless in taking care of your kids.

In this book, I'm asking a lot of you as parents. It's not easy to stay detached when your child's emotions are high and out of control. It's not always easy to patiently listen to kids without interrupting or correcting their information and logic. It can be challenging to follow through with your agreements and hold kids accountable. It's difficult to let go and watch your kids be frustrated, make mistakes or bad decisions, fail, struggle or be unhappy. Sometimes, it can be hard to say no, and it can be taxing to not engage our teenagers who are baiting us and pushing our buttons. *My teenage daughter just walked into my room and said, "Mom, if you take my hairbrush, can you please remember to put it back?". I just looked at her and laughed and laughed and laughed until she slowly backed out of the room.*

You will need to be present and disciplined to stay disengaged from your child's drama. You will need to stay very aware of your hot buttons and your feelings in order to not add your feelings and "baggage' to your child's emotions. You will need to stay focused on the long-term benefits of your discipline model when it comes time to follow through on agreements or to say no and stick with it when it's important.

You will need to stay calm when your children can't or won't. Someone has got to be the adult in those situations when your kids are losing it. That someone is us. As much as I admire, respect and believe in the ability of teenagers, sometimes even the best of them loses it. We discussed previously that the parts of their brains that manage impulse control, decision-making and abstract thinking are still developing throughout the teen years. In those moments we must become their prefrontal cortex and remain emotionally regulated when they are not.

To pull off all the aforementioned feats, parents must be calm, focused and disciplined. That can only happen if you have been taking care of your physical, emotional, social and spiritual needs. If you put those needs last on your to-do list, most days you will never get to it. When you have kids of any age, there is always something going on that requires your attention, be it dirty diapers, homework, friendship dramas or teens driving at nighttime.

You've got to make taking care of yourself important! The same goes for your marriage. I see so many young couples who have been married seven years and have two young children begin to slowly but surely drift apart. Any relationship left untended suffers. Resentments build up and couples start to feel more distant. It is all preventable.

When it comes to taking care of yourself, make sure what you do is fulfilling, i.e., refuels you. Watching TV, playing video games, or scouring social media to me are not "refuelers." They distract you from your problems and zone you out. That's different from activities that energize you and leave you feeling calmer and more refreshed.

For your physical well-being, think in terms of regular exercise. This could look like working out at a gym three to four times per week. Or it could look like taking walks with your kids around the neighborhood. I encourage parents to find a middle-school-aged kid down the street to come to their house and babysit their kids for an hour, two or three days a week at the bewitching hours (4- 6 p.m.) so mom and dad can take a walk together. It's well worth paying some kid $5-$10 for an hour of "me"-time. Or hire a sitter and take a nap, go to a class, walk with a friend, etc.

Years ago, I started playing basketball at our church with the over-thirty gang. I did that on Tuesday nights for about 20 years. At first, I seemed to miss half of the weeks because I'd have a talk or class scheduled, and I'd blame my wife or my day timer. Then, I decided to be proactive. I would look ahead a year in advance and mark off Tuesday evenings so that if someone called wanting me to give a talk, I'd remember to keep Tuesday nights free.

Running full-court basketball for 1-2 hours was a great stress reliever for me; there's nothing like a good sweat! But I had to make it important and plan ahead, or it wouldn't happen. So must you.

When my sister Jenny had three young children, she'd wake up at 5:30 a.m. every day and run for 45 minutes while her husband was still home. She made running important, significant enough to get up early every day. And she was asleep most nights by 9-9:30 p.m. in order to make it happen and get enough rest.

As far as your emotional and spiritual needs are concerned, make it a habit to incorporate these types of activities into your schedule. Look for yoga and tai chi classes in your community. Learn how to meditate and do it every morning.

I went on a weekend retreat with a friend out in Petaluma, CA, years ago that taught us how to meditate. I've never regretted it. Most mornings, I take some quiet time to meditate, usually 15-30 minutes. This quiet time sets the tone for my day and keeps me overall more peaceful and even keeled. The place I went to is called the Blue Mountain Center of Meditation, which you can reach at 800-475-2369 or www.NILGIRI.org. They have a catalog loaded with great self-quieting books and tapes.

Make it a habit to start reading some new spiritual books. Read biographies of great spiritual teachers from all different religions. Browse the new age section of your bookstore. Look for classes at your local colleges on meditation and yoga. Fill your spiritual cup however, it works for you.

Don't forget your social needs. Make time to hang out with people who are positive and who are giving and fun vs. people who are negative and suck energy from everyone. There is nothing more therapeutic and stress relieving than an evening laughing deeply with good friends. Laughter really is the best medicine.

You can read lots of books about simplifying your life and about taking care of yourself. Put it into practice and make solid commitments to yourself, or it won't happen.

Lastly, you've got to find time to nurture your relationship with your spouse. And again, you *must* make it a priority, or it too won't happen: candlelit dinners after kids are asleep, foot massages while sitting together on the couch watching movies, taking long walks together or lounging in the bathtub or hot tub. Pick whatever fits for you and your spouse. Go on couple's retreats to keep learning more tools for communication and to renew your love for each other.

I have seen too many couples grow apart due to spending so much time and energy directed at their children and little for each other. When the last child leaves the nest, these parents look at each other like, "Who are you?" Some go on to divorce, while others take on the task of renewing their relationship. But it is preventable if you make nurturing your marriage a priority all along the way.

I kidnapped my wife Anne on our 10-year wedding anniversary with a surprise trip to Kauai, Hawaii. I took care of all the details, including having her parents watch our three kids. I wouldn't divulge where we were going until we reached the gate. It was an amazing getaway. On the trip, we decided to buy a timeshare to ensure that we would take a fun vacation together every year. It was a commitment to our marriage. We're going on 43 years of marriage and 33 yearly trips.

I read somewhere about a couple who take a vacation together every year. Wherever they go, they do a ceremony to renew their vows using the culture they are visiting. They've had ceremonies on beaches, mountain tops, temples and castles. Sounds like a great tradition to me.

In the back of the book, I have listed some resources that will guide you towards finding the ways that best fit your personality and needs as far as filling your cup. Make it important. Make it a priority. And notice how much more effective you are as a parent when you and your marriage are in good order.

Chapter 18

Odds and Ends

There are several issues that I chose not to cover in depth in this book, not because they weren't important, but because they deserve more in-depth discussion and because there are already some great resources out there covering these areas.

In this chapter I will touch briefly on several issues and then give you my favorite resources for you to turn to for more information should you desire it.

Spirituality

This is obviously a critical area for anyone who wants to feel grounded, at peace and fulfilled. Spirituality in a family can look like prayers at meals and bedtime, church services, youth groups, religious retreats, or reading Bible stories.

I've also come to believe that spirituality encompasses personal growth. Understanding yourself and what makes you tick. Spirituality can look like understanding and reframing any old, limiting beliefs you've brought along with you from childhood that are negatively affecting your behavior and relationships. Anything that allows you to be fully present and fully you.

It also encompasses teaching kids about being honest and using integrity. It involves discussions about morality and knowing what's right and making choices that are in alignment with what you believe and value.

'Your life may be the only Bible your children ever read."

I love that quote as it reminds me of the importance of what I model for my kids by how I live my life. We know from experience that children become who we are, not what we tell them to be. We need to be constantly aware of what we are saying, how we are treating ourselves and others, how we manage our successes and failures and how we talk about ourselves. Let me give you a couple of real-life examples of what I'm talking about.

I have a friend who was having an intense conversation about sexuality with his two teenage daughters one night at the dinner table. His 16-year-old daughter mentioned that one of the girls in her class had just found out that she was pregnant. During the ensuing conversation, my friend said something to the effect that it didn't surprise him as that girl had always been kind of a "slut."

I can imagine the disappointed look on his daughter's face. Unwittingly, what her dad had just told her was that it wasn't safe to talk about sex, dating and boys in their home. He was too judgmental. If his daughter had had any doubts about whether it was safe to talk to her dad about boys and relationships, they were dispelled quickly after that conversation.

There are lots of opportunities, starting when children are young, to talk about sexuality in a nonjudgmental, open way. I've had some incredibly open and frank discussions about dating and sexuality in group therapy settings and at our high school camps. Our staff does a great job of listening and giving teens new ways of looking at those issues that they think about and question their choices and decisions and options. Unfortunately, my friend modeled to his daughters that it wasn't safe to be honest with him.

One time when my son TJ was about 10 years old, I flew to another city and then had a long three-hour drive to my final destination. My back had been tight and sore recently so when I got off the plane, I took one of their pillows for back support for the long car ride.

My son T.J. noticed the pillow when I returned home from the trip and asked where I got it. I told him I took it from the airplane, and being as intense and bright as he is, he questioned my integrity. I admitted I shouldn't have taken it and that I had made a mistake, and I told him I would pay the airline for it the next time I flew.

Well, I thought the incident was over, but little did I know how great my son's memory was. The following year, he and I were in the grocery store, and he took a cookie from the cookie bin. I gave him a funny look and said something sarcastically about his integrity, and he immediately came back with a comment about my taking the pillow from the airline! He was, in essence, saying that since I had been out of integrity, I couldn't call him out when he was out of integrity.

I gently refuted his logic, but it was a great, not-so-gentle reminder to me about the powerful impact of my modeling. As parents, we've got to walk the talk, because kids, especially teens, are very sensitive to double standards. If I want my kids to have good morals and live in integrity, I certainly must live out all that I want to see in them.

The following are some of my favorite books on bringing spirituality into your home.

- *Awareness*, Anthony DeMello. Doubleday, 1990
- *10 Principles for Spiritual Parenting*, Mimi Doe, Harper Perennial, 1998.
- *The Moral Life of Children*, Robert Coles, Houghton Mifflin Company, 1986
- *Right From Wrong: Instilling a Sense of Integrity in Your Child*, Mike Riera, Perseus Publishing, 2002.
- *Buddha Never Raised Kids & Jesus Didn't Drive Carpool: Seven Principles for Parenting with Soul*, Vickie Falcone, Jodere Group, 2003.
- *The Seven Spiritual Laws for Parents*, Deepak Chopra, Harmony Books, 1997.

Divorce

Again, this topic needs a lot more attention than one chapter. Going through a separation and/or a divorce has profound effects on everyone, including children, parents and the family unit. There are many tools contained in this book that are invaluable in helping families and children stay grounded during and after a divorce.

Family meetings are a godsend to divorced families. Have them all together or as two separate households. Talking through the rules and expectations at both houses clears up confusion and misunderstandings, which are common. It also allows stepparents to get clear with everyone about their role in the parenting and discipline process. Girls in my counseling practice tell me all the time that one of the hardest adjustments they have had to cope with following a separation or divorce was going between two houses.

Keeping your goodwill account full is also of vital importance as everyone works through their feelings and concerns. Kids need to feel loved, important, heard and understood no matter how sad or stressed parents become. It's hard not to be distracted when you, as a parent, are working through your own emotions from the divorce, as well as the feelings associated with a new love if you are dating or remarrying. But your kids need you, and they need you to be present and emotionally available. Making regular deposits into the GWA throughout a crisis like a divorce helps everyone continue to feel connected, loved and secure.

The following are some good books to help parents best support their children through divorce.

- *Helping Your Kids Cope with Divorce* by M. Gary Neuman
- *Second Chances: Men, Women and Children a Decade after Divorce* by Judith Wallerstein

Intrinsic Motivation vs. Externals

One of my biggest concerns about kids today is that they are inundated with externals: bribes and rewards for good behaviors, punishments for bad behavior, materialistic values and lookism. Kids are conditioned to look outside of themselves to their peers, the media, celebrities and the culture for their sense of themselves, i.e., Am I okay? Do I look okay? Am I too fat? What does success mean? What do I need to make me happy? As I discussed in chapter 15, we aren't teaching kids how to look within for their motivation and answers to important questions.

And the cost is high. People directed by externals are unfulfilled, discontented and unhappy. They tend to have problems with addictions, balance and relationships.

The following resources will give you great insights, awareness, and tools for guiding children to become internally directed.

- *Punished by Rewards: The Trouble with Gold Stars, Incentive Plans, A's, Praise and Other Bribes* by Alfie Kohn
- *Awareness* by Anthony DeMello
- *The High Price of Materialism* by Tim Kasser
- *Drive*, by Daniel Pink

Family Mission Statement

Anne and I have run some "Family Camps" over the years and one of the most important processes we take families through during the weekend is developing a family mission statement. Taking the time to slow down as a family and get clear about what's really important to them is incredibly valuable. It's a way of setting the tone for the home together.

As a result of creating a family mission statement, families can decide what their family's purpose is, what their family is all about, what principles their family most values, how everyone wants to feel at home, how they want to treat each other, what are their family's highest priorities and goals, what are the principles that they want to guide them, and how their family can contribute to society.

The process of arriving at a family mission statement is probably more valuable than the final product itself. It will require active listening, looking inward, respecting each other's opinions, everyone feeling safe to participate fully, everyone feeling heard and valuable, and coming together as a family.

The final product can look like a picture, a poem, a symbol or coat of arms, a motto, or a written statement. Having a shared vision creates a lot of closeness as well as a guidepost to refer to for the rest of your family's life together.

The following resources will help to guide you towards creating a mission statement for your family.

- *The 7 Habits of Highly Effective Families* by Stephen Covey
- *The 7 Habits of Highly Effective Families Leadership Application Workbook* by Stephen Covey
- *Your Fondest Dream* by Jim Leonard

Parent's Personal Growth

For many families that I counsel, the limiting factor in parents being more effective is not a lack of knowledge or effective tools, it is their "baggage." What I mean by baggage is what old beliefs, unresolved feelings and issues we bring with us when we become parents.

All of us bring old feelings and old beliefs from our past. Some of those beliefs are healthy, i.e., "I deserve to take care of myself, I deserve to set boundaries, I am not responsible for everyone's happiness, intimacy feels good, I believe in myself."

But some of the beliefs aren't healthy or beneficial for our parenting, i.e., "I'm responsible for everyone's happiness, conflict is bad, what I have to say isn't important, everyone else's needs are more important than mine or I shouldn't have needs,

I don't deserve to set boundaries or take care of myself, I have to do everything myself or it won't be done right, I have little self-confidence and thus will be overly influenced by what others say and think about me and I'll have a hard time trusting my gut with parenting."

The decisions we have made about ourselves, life, relationships, intimacy, men, women and the world will play a huge role in how effectively we parent. Often, we aren't aware of these decisions consciously. Nonetheless, they drive our actions.

Old unresolved feelings can have the same effect. These can be feelings from having experiences growing up where you felt neglected, abandoned, unloved, or unimportant; where you were physically, emotionally or sexually abused, felt left out or excluded socially, were teased or bullied, were criticized or judged a lot or went through crises such as divorce, death, terror, trauma, moves or poverty. Most adults never really worked through their emotions, reframed any limiting beliefs, or forgave people who hurt them.

Someday I will write an entire book on this subject because of how strongly I feel it affects our parenting. There are many kids who are "vulnerable children"— vulnerable to being treated differently because of feelings that parents bring from their own past. This includes feelings evoked because of issues with that child, including infertility, premature birth, health concerns, problems with feeding or weight gain, or any issue that causes parents to see that child differently than they are. I call these "ghosts in the nursery," a phrase that was coined years ago by the psychiatrist Selma Fraiberg, author of *The Magic Years.* Ghosts are any feelings or beliefs from the parent's past or feelings or worries from the child's early life that can come back to 'haunt' your parenting.

In the bibliography, I have listed some of my favorite personal growth books. It can be invaluable for parents to also commit

themselves to a path of personal growth and self-discovery through:
- personal growth retreats
- spiritual or personal growth book groups
- counseling
- spiritual growth
- learning self-quieting skills

The more you know yourself and know what makes you tick, especially as far as your parenting goes, the more effective spouse and parent you will become. You will be parenting more consciously vs. being constantly pulled on and influenced by subconscious feelings and beliefs. Oftentimes when our kids trigger us, it's because they are activating old emotions, i.e., ghosts, that we never handled, making us vulnerable to parenting differently or overreacting to the present moment's experiences. It is common for adults to have stuffed old, unresolved feelings and experiences that remain hidden for years. These unconscious emotions are often triggered and brought to the surface in our relationships with our spouse or children.

Your children will always be a reflection of you and your marriage. The more centered, balanced and happy you are, the more likely your children and family will become grounded when the outside world is flying by the seat of its pants.

Chapter 19

What's Really Important

"Why should we be in such desperate haste to succeed, and in such desperate enterprises? If a man does not keep pace with his companions, perhaps it is because he hears a different drummer. Let him step to the music which he hears, however measured or far away." ~ Henry David Thoreau

We've bought a lie in this country, lock, stock and barrel. I'm talking about the falsehood that says that what's really important is being rich, famous, winning, being the best, fitting in, being popular, being thin, never growing old, having the right body and the most "stuff."

Our kids are being inundated with these lies, bombarded from all sides. Television sitcoms, reality TV, music videos, song lyrics, movies, social media, and advertising all point kids in this unhealthy direction. Many adults are modeling these unhealthy messages as well.

Five-year-olds who start kindergarten not yet reading are labeled 'behind' and placed in remedial classes. First- and second-graders not already playing on a select soccer team are considered behind and at risk for not making their high school team. Eight-year-olds are having to go through six tryouts to make an ice hockey team. Young kids in grade school are traveling around the country, competing in tournaments and vying for national championships. It's absurd and it sends the wrong message to kids.

We are telling kids that it's all about winning and being #1. We are teaching kids that what's important is looking good and being special and acquiring more "things." Materialism and lookism are two of the many new "gods" that kids and adults worship today…and become addicted to.

We've gained the world but lost our souls. Every religion, in its own words, has warned us about this problem. But we are running so fast and are so distracted and disconnected from our kids, ourselves and reality that we can't see the forest for the trees. Most families seem too caught up in the rat race to have any awareness of how much it is costing them.

In his book *The High Price of Materialism,* Tim Kasser has put together decades of research documenting the cost to teens and adults when their lives are focused on materialistic pursuits. The following is a summary of some of Kasser's findings.

1. Even aspiring to have greater wealth and material possessions makes people more likely to have increased personal unhappiness, increased anxiety, increased risk of depression, increased somatic complaints, watching more TV, using more alcohol and drugs, having poorer relationships, and having dreams with more anxiety and distress.

2. Once above the poverty line, gains in wealth have no incremental payoffs in terms of happiness and well-being.

3. Teens and adults who were focused on financial vs. non-materialistic values had lower psychological well-being, lower levels of self-actualization and vitality, significantly higher levels of stress, depression and anxiety, more difficulty adjusting to life, less positive emotions and exhibited more behavior disorders compared to teens focused on other values (self-acceptance, service, community, etc.).

4. Materialistic teenagers were more likely to engage in cigarette smoking, chewing tobacco, alcohol, pot and sexual intercourse and to have increased difficulties with attention, social isolation, expressing emotions and controlling their impulses. They were either avoidant or overly dependent on other people, attempted to over control many aspects of their

environment, and related to people in a passive-aggressive manner.

5. Adults and college students who strongly focused on the pursuit of wealth, fame and image reported a lower quality of relationships with friends and lovers, relationships that were shorter, less positive and more negative; more conflictual and aggressive behaviors in dating relationships; greater feelings of alienation and separateness from society, a devaluing of close, intimate relationships and community involvement, and little empathy and generosity in relationships.

These studies were done cross-culturally, some with as many as 40 countries evaluated. Materialistic values were things such as financial success, fame and popularity and physical attractiveness, i.e., externals. Non-materialistic values were self-acceptance and personal growth, intimacy and friendship, and societal contributions. This is great research backing up what we've known for thousands of years: that the focus on and the pursuit of externals doesn't fulfill people in a healthy and lasting way.

So, what **is** really important? What values and ideals should kids aspire towards? The following are some ideals I think kids should strive for, learning and being modeled by parents.

To know how to give and receive love

It's important to know how to acknowledge others, support others the way they want to be supported and to give affection appropriately. Lots of teenagers I work with in our retreats and summer camps have no clue how to be close to peers, especially after their experiences with the global pandemic. Teens and young adults tell me they feel much more socially awkward than they used to. They know how to be sexual but not how to be loving, nurturing and affectionate.

I also want kids to be able to take in love and nurturing, to be able to accept acknowledgments. I know a lot of adults who have a hard time taking in affirmations because they feel they don't deserve it or they don't believe it. They suffer because of it. The start of family meetings was one place where you could regularly give and receive acknowledgments from your family.

Be content with who you are

It is essential that kids know and love themselves. They need to understand their strengths, weaknesses and what makes them tick. And they need to learn to accept and love themselves for exactly who they are, warts and all.

Kids who know and like themselves are less at risk for being teased and excluded, and they don't take on teasing and criticism if it happens. I encourage girls and young women I work with to first learn to love and accept themselves, and that becomes the impetus for self-care. They will be less likely to get caught up in the rat race of constantly trying to impress others and prove themselves. They can use the self-quieting skills we discussed in chapter 15 to be in touch with their feelings, thoughts and desires.

Personal awareness, personal growth, self-reflection and a rich inner life are essential for people to feel fulfilled and happy. Kids at younger and younger ages are getting caught up in the self-dissatisfaction and discontent so prevalent in adults. The cosmetic industry and plastic surgery businesses are booming today as adults and teenagers fight aging and feelings of dissatisfaction. It's important that kids grow up knowing and loving themselves.

Know how to lift others up and make everyone on their team successful

There is so much emphasis today on winning and being #1 that we've forgotten that what's really important is to help others be successful.

We do an exercise at our camps called "TowwJam," which stands for Together-We-Win-Jamboree. This exercise allows kids to experience what it feels like when everyone on a team cares about each other and pulls together.

Recently, my wife Anne and I had a 5th grade class who had a reputation for being overly competitive do the TOWWJAM exercise. We divided them up into four groups of five kids each, with the task of seeing who could make the most free throws (throwing tennis balls into trash cans twelve feet away) in 30 seconds.

In the first round, we said the intention was to see who could make the most free throws. What we saw is the same thing I've seen dozens of times working with kids, teens, adults and corporations. There was little, if any, support or encouragement, and the shooters were basically on their own to retrieve missed shots and to shoot. The winner made 6 free throws, and the total score from all four groups combined was 44 free throws made.
When we asked the class how they felt, most kids said it was okay but not very fun because a lot of them hadn't made many baskets or gotten any help.

We then re-did the game, but this time changed the intention from who can make the most free throws to three different purposes:
- Make sure everyone on the team is wildly successful
- Have fun
- Do your personal best during your turn to shoot

We brainstormed how they could accomplish the new intentions, huddled with their small groups to discuss strategies to support each other, and the entire team recommitted to a new goal of 50 free throws. Only then did they start shooting.

The results, as always, were amazing. The kids were laughing and having a much better time. They were focused on supporting each shooter. And when we regrouped at the end, they were all smiles. And, they made 78 shots!

More important than the number was how they felt. They all felt so much happier and fulfilled because their interest was outward, making sure everyone felt successful. Having experienced the difference in TOWWJAM hopefully will motivate and inspire kids as to what's really important when it comes to the classroom, playing games at recess, and life.

Relationship with your spouse someday

All kids deserve to live in a home where parents model a healthy relationship. It's vital that kids see parents being affectionate with each other, resolving conflicts peacefully, cooperating, and expressing love. It's their parent's relationship that gives them the template for their own dating and spousal relationships later on in life.

Live a life of service and giving

Kids need opportunities to experience the good feelings and fulfillment that come from being of service to others. Those feelings are the real deal, not the superficial transient highs you get from being popular or winning a game or buying a new outfit.

Kids can experience the fulfillment derived from service by being helpful at home, collecting money for charities, tithing, or doing volunteer work out in the community. The more they experience being of service, see their parents modeling being of service and hear stories of people who devoted their lives to service, the more kids will internalize the importance of it. Watch movies or read books about people like Martin Luther King, Gandhi and Mother Teresa or your favorite service "heroes."

Finally, what might be more important for kids to learn is how to find their passions, what fulfills them, their purpose in life, and to go after it with all of their energies.

One of the most impactful questions you can ask a child is why they like the activities that they do. Here are some examples of how this could sound:
- *What do you like about the picture you colored?*
- *What kind of grades do you want and why?*
- *What do you love so much about playing your sport?*
- *Why do you like acting in plays?*
- *Do you have any idea what you might like to pursue after you graduate high school?*

Once you ask the question, sit back and listen attentively because your child will go inward and express what those things mean to them. A 5-year-old is likely to tell you they liked how they used all of the colors in the box in their artwork. Adults might have said that they liked how they colored in the lines this time.

I asked 6th grader Sophia what she liked so much about gymnastics that she was willing to practice six days a week. Her parents were sure it was all of the blue ribbons and trophies she had won. Sophia instead described how much she loved her floor routine. "I love being on the mat all by myself, with all eyes on me. I am so in the moment and block everything out, and for those few moments, it's pure joy for me."

The typical response I get from girls I counsel about what grades they want to earn is, "Well, A's." If the dumbfounded expression on their face could talk, it would proclaim, "Duh, what do you think I want?" When I follow up by asking why do you want As, then it gets interesting. Many girls will rattle off a mantra about how they want to get good grades in high school so they can be admitted into a top college. When I ask why they want to go to a top university, they tell me so they'll be able to get a good job, and the reason for a good job is to make a lot of money. Think back to the earlier research by Tim Kasser that revealed the unhealthy outcomes for people focused on externals.

The other more common response to my question about why they want to attend college is…pause…and…crickets. They don't have an answer because no one has ever asked them why *they* might want to go to college. Most girls I work with are making choices about grades, activities, and college to please their parents or to not disappoint them. There is also the reason of everyone else is going and, at their high school, it's expected that all grads go to college. This is one of the main reasons I encourage kids to develop the ability to be alone and quiet, and to rely on their intuition to know what's right for them; to get clear about *their* reasons for all that they do.

I want teens and young adults to spend time reflecting and journaling about questions such as: "Any ideas about what you might want to be when you grow up?" "What's your dream?" "What's your purpose for being on this planet?" They don't need to have all of the answers as young women, but I do want them to get comfortable at checking in with themselves and knowing what's best and right for them at each stage of their life.

We need to guide them in aligning their strengths, passion and interests with potential careers. We need to encourage them to read biographies of people who worked in and made a difference in their field of interest. We need to find mentors, jobs and volunteer opportunities for kids that match their interests. And we, of course, need to model doing work that we love and are passionate about.

I developed a concept I call my **Dot Theory** years ago as a process for how young adults can find their calling. Most of them have done one of those connect-the-dot drawings growing up. You had no idea what the final picture would be by looking at just the dots. So, you'd start connecting them one at a time. At some point, a picture would start to emerge, and when all the dots were connected, the final image was present. This is a great metaphor for finding your calling.

I encourage young people not to feel pressured into feeling like they should know their whole life's path at age eighteen. Their job is just to be open to "dots" that cross their path. Dots are opportunities such as a class in school, a job, traveling experiences, hobbies, reading biographies of people who pursued an interest of theirs, having a cup of coffee with an adult who is working in a field they have interest in, being on sports teams or performing in theater. I encourage teens to be aware of dot experiences that cross their path that sound fun and that they are drawn to for any reason or that they get an urge to try. Not because it directly leads to a career but just because, at this moment in their life, it feels like the right thing to do. The truth is that if they do that, the dots will connect for them over time. Their life will unfold marvelously in their own way and in their own time. Instead of trying to force their life process, I want them to trust the process of life. And I tell them to interview any adult they bump into and ask them about their life path. Almost every adult I have ever questioned about their life journey experienced a zigzag course to finding their calling; it's almost never a straight line going from A directly to Z.

The above-mentioned are the values we need to live out and model and discuss in our homes. We need to more than balance out the unhealthy messages kids are getting from the culture about what's important. These are the kind of values and ideals that will allow kids to grow up feeling grounded, happy, and fulfilled no matter how much the world around them is flying by the seat of its pants.

Resources

DISCIPLINE/PARENTING

1. Jordan, Tim. *Food Fights and Bedtime Battles: A Working Parent's Guide to Negotiating Daily Power Struggles,* Berkley Books, 2001.
2. Jordan, Tim. Online parenting course: *Parenting girls: The challenges girls face today with their feelings and friends and what they need,* 2021.
3. Jordan, Tim. *Dinner Dialogue Cards: Conversation cards to get your family talking!*
4. Kvols, Kathryn J. *Redirecting Children's Behavior,* Parenting Press, 3rd edition, 1998.
5. Neville, Helen and Diane Johnson. *Temperament Tools,* Parenting Press, 1998.
6. Dreikurs, Rudolph, M.D. and Vicki Soltz, R.N. *Children: The Challenge,* E.P. Dutton, 1964.
7. Faber, Adele and Elaine Mazlish. *How to Talk So Kids Will Listen and Listen So Kids Will Talk,* New York, NY, Avon, 1982.
8. Kohn, Alfie. *Punished by Rewards: The Trouble with Gold Stars, Incentive Plans, A's, Praise and Other Bribes,* Houghton Mifflin Co., 1993.
9. Nelson, Jane. *Positive Discipline,* Ballantine Books, 1987.
10. Thompson, Michael and Dan Kindlon. *Raising Cain: Protecting the Emotional Life of Boys.*
11. Pollack, William. *Real Boys: Rescuing Our Sons from the Myths of Boyhood,* 1998.
12. Vickie Falcone. *Buddha Never Raised Kids & Jesus Didn't Drive Carpool: Seven Principles for Parenting With Soul,* Jodere Group, 2003.
13. Coles, Robert. *The Moral Life of Children,* Houghton Mifflin Co., 1986.

14. Pink, Daniel. *Drive: The Surprising Truth About What Motivates Us*
15. Flanagan, Linda. *Take Back the Game: How Money and Mania Are Ruining Kids' Sports-and Why It Matters*
16. Thompson, Michael. *Best Friends, Worst Enemies: Understanding the Social Lives of Children*

FAMILY MEETINGS

1. Covey, Stephen. *The Seven Habits of Highly Effective Families*, Golden Books, 1997.
2. Hightower, Elaine and Betsy Riley. *Our Family Meeting Book*, Free Spirit Publishing, 2002.
3. Levison, Mariah. *From Conflict to Convergence: Coming Together to Solve Tough Problems*, 2024.

TEENAGERS

1. Jordan, Tim. *Sleeping Beauties, Awakened Women: Guiding the Transformation of Adolescent Girls*, 2013.
2. Jordan, Tim. *Letters from My Grandfather: Timeless Wisdom for a Life Worth Living*, 2018.
3. Jordan, Tim. *She Leads: A Practical Guide for Raising Girls Who Advocate, Influence, and Lead*, 2020.
4. Nelson, Jane. *I'm on Your Side: Resolving Conflicts with your Teenage Son or Daughter*, Prima Publishing, 1990.
5. Meeker, Margaret. *Restoring the Teenage Soul*, McKinley and Mann, 1999.
6. Cohen-Sandler, Roni. *"I'm Not Mad, I Just Hate You!" A New Understanding of Mother-Daughter Conflict*, Penguin Books, 1999.
7. Pipher, Mary. *Reviving Ophelia*, New York, Ballantine Books, 1994.
8. Sessions Stepp, Laura. *Our Last Best Shot: Guiding Our Children Through Early Adolescence*, Riverhead Books, 2000.
9. Hersch, Patricia. *A Tribe Apart - A Journey into the Heart of American Adolescence*, Fawcett Columbine, 1998.
10. Riera, Michael. *Staying Connected to Your Teenager*

11. Riera, Michael. *Uncommon Sense for Parents with Teenagers,* Celestial Arts, 1995.
12. Bluestein, Jane. *Parents, Teens and Boundaries, Health Communications,* 1993.
13. Hine, Thomas. *The Rise and Fall of the American Teenager*
14. Bruni, Frank. *Where You Go Is Not Who You'll Be: An Antidote to the College Admissions Mania*

SOCIAL MEDIA AND TECHNOLOGIES

1. Turkle, Sherry. *Alone Together*
2. Turkle, Sherry. *Reclaiming Conversation*
3. Powers, William. *Hamlet's Blackberry: A Practical Philosophy for Building a Good Life in the Digital Age*
4. Boyd, Danah. *It's Complicated: The Social Lives of Networked Teens*
5. McGonigal, Kelly. *The Willpower Instinct*
6. Siegel, Daniel. *Brainstorm: The Power and Purpose of the Teenage Brain*
7. Haidt, Jonathon. *The Anxious Generation: How the Great Rewiring of Childhood Is Causing an Epidemic of Mental Illness,* 2024.

SCHOOLWORK

1. Kralovec, Etta and John Buell. *The End of Homework: How Homework Disrupts Families, Overburdens Children and Limits Learning,* Beacon Press, 2000.
2. Gatto, John. *A Different Kind of Teacher,* Berkley Hills Books, 2001.
3. Gatto, John. *Dumbing Us Down: The Hidden Curriculum of Compulsory Schooling,* 1992.
4. Kohn, Alfie. *The Schools Our Children Deserve,* Houghton Mifflin Co. 1993.
5. Levine, Mel. *A Mind at a Time,* Simon & Schuster, 2002.

DIVORCE

1. Neuman, M. Gary. *Helping Your Kids Cope with Divorce,* Random House, 1998.
2. Wallerstein, Judith. *Second Chances: Men, Women, and Children a Decade after Divorce,* 1989.

DEATH AND LOSS

1. Trozzi, Maria. *Talking with Children About Loss,* Perigree Books, 1999.
2. Romain, Trevor. *What on Earth Do You Do When Someone Dies,* Free Spirit 1999.

HISTORY & PHILOSOPHY OF PARENTING

1. Jordan, M.D., Tim. *What I Learned at Summer Camp About Understanding and Loving Our Children,* St. Louis Youth Camps Press, 1994.
2. Hulbert, Ann. *Raising America: Experts, Parents and a Century of Advice about Children,* Alfred Knopf Co., 2003.
3. Postman, Neil. *The Disappearance of Childhood,* Vintage Books, 1994.
4. Pipher, Mary. *The Shelter of Each Other,* Grosset- Putnam Books, 1996.
5. Hine, Thomas. *The Rise arid Fall of the American Teenager,* Avon Books, 1999.
6. Elkind, David. *The Hurried Child,* Addison-Wesley, 1981.
7. Healy, Jane. *Endangered Minds: Why Children Don't Think and What we Can Do About It,* Touchstone, 1990.
8. Hillman, James. *The Soul's Code: In Search of Character and Calling,* Random House, 1996.

SELF QUIETING

1. Easwaran, Eknath. *Meditation: A Simple 8 Point Program for Translating Ideals into Daily Life,* Nilgiri Press, 1991.
2. Kabat-Zinn, Jon. *Wherever You Go, There You Are,* Hyperion, 1994.

3. Nhat Hanh, Thick. *Peace is Every Step,* Bantam Books, 1991.
4. Murdoch, Maureen. *Spinning Inward: Using Guided Imagery with Children for* Learning, *Creativity and Relaxation,* Shambhala, 1987.
5. Thomas, Patrice. *The Power of Relaxation: Using Tai Chi and Visualization to Reduce Children's Stress.* Redleaf press, 2003.
6. Capacchione, Lucia. *The Creative Journal for Children.* Shambhala, 1989.
7. Willey, Kira. *Breathe Like a Bear: 30 mindful moments for kids to feel calm*
8. Clarke, Carolyn. *Imaginations 1 and 2: relaxation stories and guided imagery for kids*

PERSONAL GROWTH

1. DeMello, Anthony. *Awareness,* Doubleday, 1990.
2. Dyer, Wayne. *Manifest Your Destiny.*
3. Covey, Stephen. *The 7 Habits of Highly Effective People.* Fireside Books, 1989.
4. DeMello, Anthony. *The Way to Love.* Doubleday, 1991.
5. Heider, John. *The Tao of Leadership.* Humanics New Age, 1985.
6. Eswaran, Eknath. *Gandhi the Man,* Nilgiri Press, 1978.
7. Sinetar, Marsha. *Do What You Love* and *the Money Will Follow.* Dell Books 1987.
8. Hill, Napolean. *Think and Grow Rich,* Penguin Group, 1937.
9. Dalai Lama. *The Art of Happiness,* Riverhead Books, 1998.
10. Nhat Hahn, Thich. *The Heart of the Buddha's Teaching,* Parallax Press, 1998.
11. Covey, Stephen, *The 8th Habit: From Effectiveness to Greatness,* Free Press, 2004.
12. Chopra, Deepak. *The Seven Spiritual Laws for Parents,* Harmony Books, 1997.
13. Leonard, Jim. *Your Fondest Dream.*

14. Kasser, Tim. *The High Price of Materialism,* Bradford Books, 2002.
15. Levison, Mariah. *From Conflict to Convergence: Coming Together to Solve Tough Problems*
16. Hendrix, Harville. *Getting the Love You Want: A Guide For Couples*

SPIRITUALITY

1. *Awareness*, Anthony DeMello. Doubleday, 1990.
2. *10 Principles for Spiritual Parenting*, Mimi Doe, Harper Perennial, 1998.
3. *The Moral Life of Children*, Robert Coles, Houghton Mifflin Company, 1986.
4. *Right From Wrong: Instilling a Sense of Integrity in Your Child*, Mike Riera, Perseus Publishing, 2002.
5. *Buddha Never Raised Kids & Jesus Didn't Drive Carpool: Seven Principles for Parenting with Soul*, Vickie Falcone, Jodere Group, 2003.
6. *The Seven Spiritual Laws for Parents*, Deepak Chopra, Harmony Books, 1997.

About the Author

Tim Jordan, MD is a Developmental and Behavioral Pediatrician in private practice in St. Louis, Missouri, where he counsels girls from grade school through college on issues including friendships, anxiety, stress, finding purpose, school pressures, family relationships, and more. He also hosts a weekly podcast, *Raising Daughters*, is an international speaker who has spoken to parents and professionals in 17 countries, a YPO (Young Presidents Organization) resource/facilitator, and is a school and media consultant.

Dr. Jordan is also the founder/owner of Camp Weloki for Girls, running personal growth/leadership development weekend retreats and summer camps since 1991. He also works with kids in school settings to create more caring learning communities in their Strong Girls, Strong World school programs. Dr. Jordan is also a key media resource speaking on TV, podcasts, & radio shows internationally. He is the author of 6 books, the latest being *She Leads: A Practical Guide for Raising Girls Who Advocate, Influence, and Lead* about raising female leaders. Dr. Jordan also published an online parenting course: *Parenting Girls: The Challenges Girls Face Today With Their Feelings and Friends and What They Need.*

Tim's favorite "work" is when he is working directly with kids and teens in retreat-type settings at his camps and at schools. His passion and interest in working with children started at an early age with taking care of his 5 younger sisters. Dr. Jordan resides with his wife, Anne, and their dog Buddy in St. Louis Missouri. They are the proud parents of 3 adult children along with 4 grandchildren.

For information about Dr. Jordan's camp, retreats and speaking presentations, email him at Anne@drtimjordan.com or visit their website at www.drtimjordan.com.

www.ingramcontent.com/pod-product-compliance
Lightning Source LLC
Chambersburg PA
CBHW071919290426
44110CB00013B/1418